JULIE ANN GO_ _

Northmoor
through the years

Alley Cat Books

Alley Cat Books 2015
© Julie Ann Godson 2015

ISBN: 978-1523711154

New Edition

The author has asserted their moral right under
the Copyright, Designs and Patents Act, 1988,
to be identified as the author of this work.

All Rights reserved. No part of this publication may be reproduced,
copied, stored in a retrieval system, or transmitted, in any form
or by any means, without the prior written consent of the copyright holder,
nor be otherwise circulated in any form of binding or cover other than that
in which it is published and without a similar condition
being imposed on the subsequent purchaser.

A CIP catalogue record for this title is available from the British Library.

Front cover: A. R. Quinton's depiction of the crossing at Bablock Hythe
in Hilaire Belloc's *The Historic Thames*, 1907,
© Oxfordshire County Council – Oxfordshire History Centre.
Title page: A cottage in Northmoor, perhaps Causeway Cottage.
Opposite: Detail from 'A New Map of Oxfordshire Drawn from
the Latest Authorities', engraved by Thomas Conder
for *The New British Traveller* (c. 1784).

Map of Oxfordshire and surrounding area

Scale: British Statute Miles (1, 2, 3, 5, 7, 10)

Places shown include:
- Banbury, Hanwell, Drayton, Hornton, Alkerton, Shelford, Swaecliffe, Broughton, Wickham
- Bloxham, Sorbrook, Newington, Barford St. John, Hook Norton, Wigginton, Doddington
- Rolwright Stones, Little Rolwright, Shire Stones, from Shipton
- Chipping Norton, Chapel on the Heath, Gr. Yew, Upper Worton, N'th Aston, Stoke
- Churchill, Sarsden, Cornwell, Kingham, Juston, Wescot Barton, Steeple Aston, Heyford
- Spilsbury, Nether Kiddington, Glympton, Middleton S., Tackley, Ak...
- Idbury, Fyfield, Ascot, Cornbury, Charlbury, Wotton, Whitting, Bleching
- Shipton, Upper Milton, Whichwood Forrest, Swinfield Park, Woodstock
- Fenton, Pudbrook Chapel, Wilcot, North Leigh, Blenheim, Bladen, Yarnton
- Burford, Minster Lovel, Newland, Begbrook, S'th Leigh, Cu...
- Westwell, Akeman Street way, Witney, Ensham
- Brise Worton, Ducklington, Lew, Cockthorp, Stanton
- To Berk Sh, Black Burton, Stanlake
- Kenco..., Broadwell, North Mocor, Gunmer, Oxford
- Bampton, Chimley
- Isis R., Kingston Baptist, Abingdon, Culham
- Faringdon, Bristol, To Berks

Bablock Hythe

In the time of wild roses
As up Thames we travelled
Where 'mid water-reeds ravelled
The lily uncloses,

To his old shores the river
A new song was singing,
And young shoots were springing
On old roots for ever.

Dog-daisies were dancing,
And flags flamed in cluster,
On the dark stream a lustre
Now blurred and now glancing.

A tall reed down-weighing,
The sedge-warbler fluttered;
One sweet note he uttered,
Then left it soft-swaying.

By the bank's sandy hollow
My dipt oars went beating,
And past our bows fleeting
Blue-backed shone the swallow.

High woods, heron-haunted,
Rose, changed, as we rounded
Old hills greenly mounded,
To meadows enchanted.

A dream ever moulded
Afresh for our wonder,
Still opening asunder
For the stream many-folded;

Till sunset was rimming
The West with pale flushes;
Behind the black rushes
The last light was dimming;

And the lonely stream, hiding
Shy birds, grew more lonely,
And with us was only
The noise of our gliding.

In clouds of gray weather
The evening o'erdarkened,
In the stillness we hearkened;
Our hearts sang together.

Laurence Binyan (1869-1943)

Jersey cows at Stonehenge Farm, December 1962

Contents

INTRODUCTION *8*

BABLOCKHYTHE
& THE RIVER'S EDGE *10*

CHURCH ROAD
TO THE OLD POST OFFICE *24*

NORTHMOOR SCHOOL *52*

CHAPEL LANE *58*

THE RED LION TO COW LANE *64*

MORETON TO NEW BRIDGE *80*

PEOPLE AND EVENTS *92*

Romano-British settlement at Watkins Farm, excavated in the 1980s

NORTHMOOR IS NAMED for the 'moor', or marshy ground, which ran between Bablock Hythe in the north-east and the river Windrush to the west. Signs of Iron Age and Romano-British settlement have been identified in the area; a marble Roman altar was dredged from the river at Bablock Hythe in 1932, Roman coins were found at Northmoor Lock, and an Iron Age sword came out of the river at New Bridge. But, perhaps because of wetter conditions, there appears to have been a gap in the occupation of the area during the early and middle Anglo-Saxon period.

Then in 1059 land in Northmoor was granted by Edward the Confessor to the Abbey of St Denis in Paris. The rest of Northmoor was acquired by the abbey before the mid 12th century, and the prefix 'North', distinguishing More from Southmoor beyond the river, was added intermittently from the late 13th century. Owing to the boggy nature of much of the farmland, the village was not always the prosperous place it is today, and the local blanket industry offered an extra income to rural households otherwise dependent on a hard-pressed agricultural economy. Electricity was introduced before 1939, mains water after 1945, and main drainage in the 1970s.

This little book was produced to support *Northmoor through the years*, a fund-raising exhibition of images of the village past and present organised by Anne Brunner-Ellis in 2011. Four years later we find ourselves once more in the throes of fund-raising—this time in aid of repairs to the chancel roof of our 13th-century church. The book does not pretend to offer a comprehensive history of every aspect of the village since the content has been led largely by the pictures kindly made available for the original exhibition by current and former residents.

Particular mention must be made of the multi-talented Graham Wren, cowman at Stonehenge Farm during the 1960s and 70s and Associate of the Royal Photographic Society. His luminous colour photographs of 'ordinary' people doing 'ordinary' jobs remind us that nothing stays the same for long, and we should all be heartily thankful that there comes among us occasionally one of those keen types with a camera perpetually slung about their necks who do us the great service of telling us to stand still while they record what feels to us unremarkable at the time.

We become so attached to our local traditions and stories that dabbling in the waters of a village's past might be considered impertinent. While the splendid *Glimpses of Northmoor through 800 years* by the Reverend J. H. Stowell (published 1931) and subsequent similar private publications have proved inspirational, I have relied most on those two great and unsentimental authorities, the *Victoria County History* and *The buildings of England: Oxfordshire* by Nikolaus Pevsner.

Julie Ann Godson
November 2015

Bablockhythe
and the river's edge

A. R. Quinton's depiction of the crossing at Bablock Hythe in Hilaire Belloc's *The Historic Thames*, 1907

EARLY VISITORS to Northmoor would have crossed the river at Bablockhythe ('the landing-place by Babba's Brook') where a ferry operated by 1212. Records show that John de la More held 30 acres of land and a passage, or ferry, over the Thames at 'Bablake' on payment of four shillings and eightpence to the Prior of Osney.

By 1279 the ferryman was John Cocus, paying a rent of 31 shillings to the Prior of Deerhurst. John de Ken in his turn negotiated a reduced rent of 20 shillings in return for maintaining the road for a distance of one and a half leagues, and allow-ing free passage to the Priors of Deerhurst.

A causeway to the ferry was mentioned from 1320, when it was said to be frequently damaged by floods. In 1692 the ferry was described as 'a great boat to carry over carts and coaches', and in 1812 regular river trade was done at the spot by a 70-ton barge, the 'Mary'. A private attempt to build a road bridge in 1855 failed following opposition from the earl of Abingdon who feared losing tolls at Swinford bridge near Eynsham. In the early 20th century no ferry ran at night or during the frequent high floods and har-nessed horses were sometimes drowned but, despite repeated local appeals for a bridge, the ferry continued until the 1960s when the crossing was at last abandoned.

In the 1950s the ferryman was a Polish refugee named John. He operated the ferry from 8 o'clock in the morning until 11 o'clock at night. Inset: Hazel and Roy Pascoe's wedding reception on the ferry in March 1959

11

The original inn was sited
on the present parking area
© Oxfordshire County Council – Oxfordshire History Centre

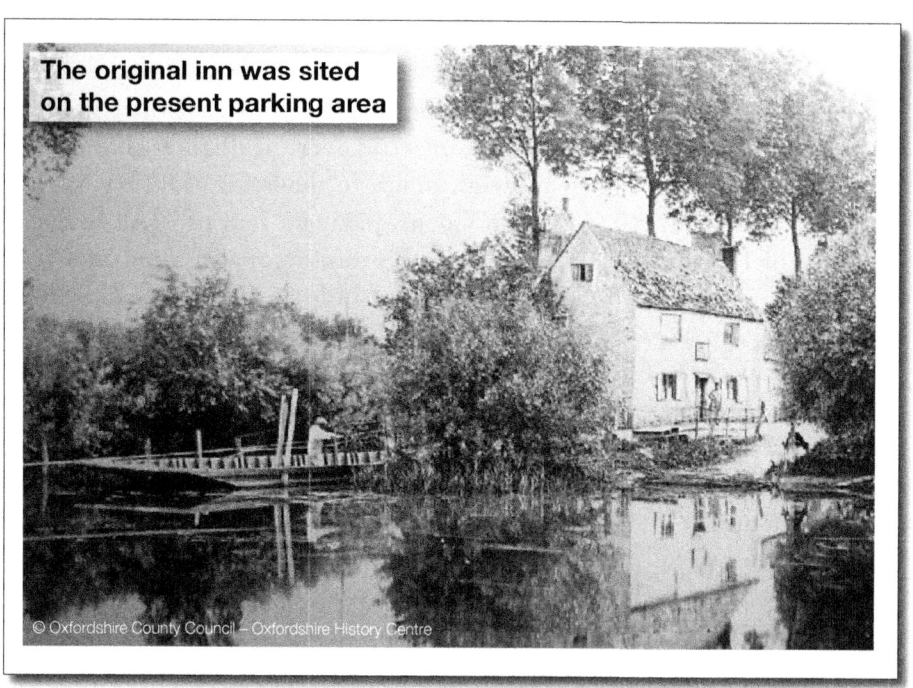

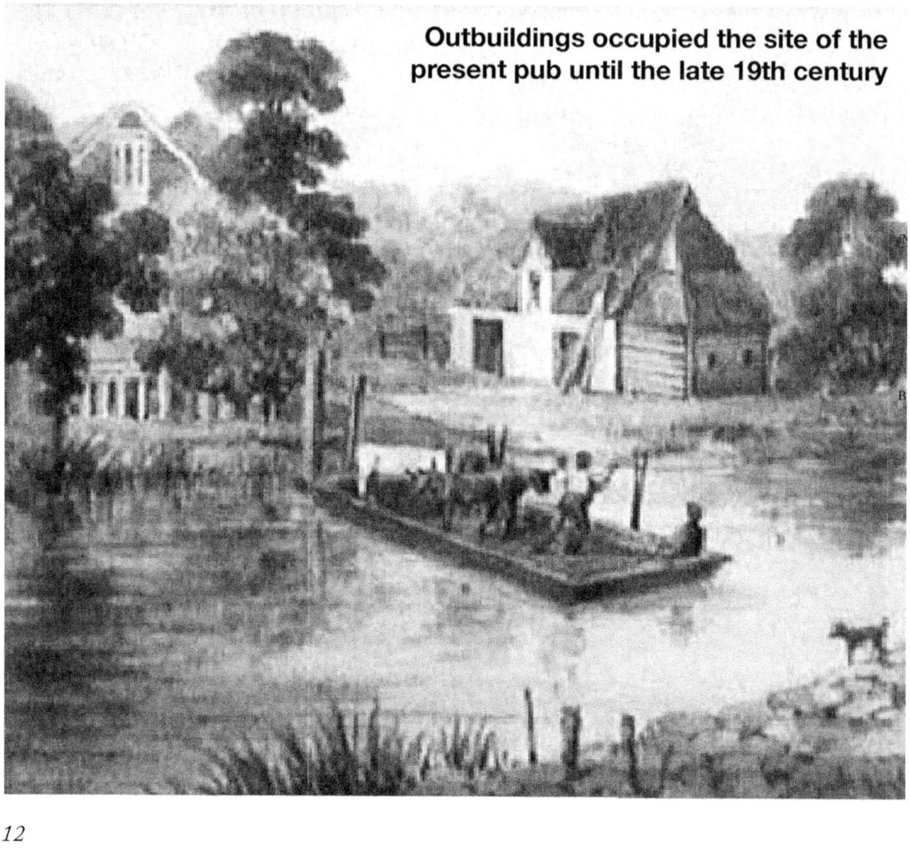
Outbuildings occupied the site of the
present pub until the late 19th century

An alehouse stood on the present parking area by the 1750s, and was 'much frequented by the lower class' in the 1850s. Later in the 19th century the Chequers stood on the site of the present pub. That building burned down in the 1930s and was replaced by the present Ferryman Inn.

In the 19th century the Chequers stood on the site of the present pub. It burned down in the 1930s

The Chequers was run during the 50s by Munro Stevenson and his wife Eleanor

JACKSON's OXFORD JOURNAL.

January 21st 1860

MELANCHOLY OCCURRENCE.—About Christmas time a man, named Hart, formerly under-porter at New College, went to visit some friends at Bablock Hythe, a few miles from Oxford, and, on his taking leave of them, they gave him two half-sovereigns. He started on his way home, but never reached it, and was heard no more of until Thursday, when he was discovered drowned in the river, near the public-house called "Noah's Ark," about half a mile on this side of Bablock Hythe. It is supposed that he missed his way and fell into the river. When the body was found his features could scarcely be distinguished, but upon him were found the two half-sovereigns which his friends had given him.

June 27th 1885

ACCIDENTALLY DROWNED.—An inquest was held on Saturday the 20th inst., before F. Westell, Esq., at the house of William Goodman, Northmoor, on the body of George Trinder.—James Webb, of Northmoor, said he knew the deceased; his name was George Trinder, of Northmoor, labourer, aged 21. About half-past nine on Thursday night he was with the deceased at this house, together with Douglas and John Cooper. We four got into a punt and went up the river. When we got about two hundred yards Douglas and deceased began larking together. He was rowing, when Cooper cried out "He's overboard, but I have got him all-right." He stopped the boat, and saw Cooper with Trinder's hat in his hand. He and Cooper stayed there in the boat for about half-an-hour watching to see if they could see Trinder, but could see nothing of him. Deceased and Douglas were rolling in the well in front of him, but he was looking back to see his road, and therefore did not see Trinder fall out of the boat. Cooper was rowing behind Trinder and Douglas. There was no quarrelling.—After hearing the evidence of Jesse Cooper and P.C. Barton, the Jury returned a verdict of "Accidentally drowned."

June 15th 1889

DISCOVERY OF THE MISSING OXFORD RESIDENT.

In last week's *Journal* a notice was inserted by the Police that an Oxford resident had been missing since the evening of the 4th inst., and in consequence of his having on the evening of that day posted two letters, the gravest suspicions were entertained as to what had become of him. Interest in the matter increased when it was known that the gentleman missing was Mr. Adin Williams, aged 54, of 33, St. Aldate's, formerly a tailor carrying on business in the High-street; he was last seen in this city on the date above-mentioned, when he appeared in a somewhat better state mentally and physically than he had been for some time past; he had been discharged from an asylum in December. Search was made for him, but unsuccessfully, and nothing was heard of him until Saturday last, when his body was found in the river near to Bablock Hythe. On the afternoon of that day, Mr. Cecil Walsh, of St. John's College, son of Mr. Percival Walsh, solicitor, was picnicing on the upper river, and one boat containing a number of ladies had passed the Ferry, when Mr. Walsh, who was following, noticed something in the water. On looking more closely he saw that it was the body of a man; it was entirely under water, and about 150 yards above Bablock Hythe, near the Berkshire shore. The ferryman and his son were communicated with, and they visited the spot, and information having been given to the police at Appleton, the body was got out of the water. A handkerchief was tied over the eyes, and a relative who happened to be near identified the body as that of the missing Mr. Williams.

March 25th 1899

ESCAPE OF AN UNDER-GRADUATE.

DRIVING INTO THE RIVER.

On Friday afternoon an occurrence of an alarming character took place at Bablock-hythe Ferry, near Stanton-Harcourt, in which an undergraduate of New College had a narrow escape from death, and a valuable horse was drowned. It appears that there was a meet of the Christ Church Beagles in the neighbourhood, and that the gentleman in question, Mr. M. A. Sands, drove there in an American four-wheel trotting waggon, which he hired of Mr. F. W. Hedderley, livery stable keeper, of the Clarendon Hotel yard. Accounts differ as to the real cause of the mishap, but Mr. Sands drove into the river, thinking probably that it was fordable, instead of making use of the ferry-boat, and at once found himself in from twelve to fourteen feet of water. He succeeded in scrambling out at the back part of the vehicle and getting safely to the bank, but the horse and waggon sank immediately, and did not come again to the surface, through getting under the ferry boat, which, as is well known, is a broad and heavy craft. Assistance arrived, and after a considerable time had elapsed the carcase and the vehicle were hauled to the bank. The horse was estimated to be worth from 50gs. to 60gs. Mr. Sands obtained a change of clothing at the inn at the ferry, and appeared shortly afterwards, to be none the worse for his involuntary ducking.

15

The stretch of low-lying land between Bablockhythe and the Windrush used to be subject to flooding almost every year so that in 1866, on the initiative of local farmers and landowners, the Northmoor and Stanton Harcourt Drainage Board was established under the Land Drainage Act of 1861. Several miles of embankments and cuttings were constructed along the river Thames and a short stretch of the river Windrush. Houses in the village had previously been damp and unhealthy, but in 1870 Northmoor's appearance was said to have changed completely as a result of the drainage works. In the 20th century the Thames Conservancy Board undertook further improvements to the flood bank that runs through the fields some half a mile south of the village.

The river path from Bablockhythe to Moreton would once have served a string of hamlets making up a considerable population and considered at the time to be part of Moreton. Just up-river from Bablockhythe is a small, boat-shaped island created by a spasmodic stream which leaves and then rejoins the river. Appropriately named Noah's Ark, the island was once the site of Ark's weir. In 1841 there were two farmhouses and four labourers' cottages there, but only faint traces remained by 1910.

Between this and the next weir lay a straggle of cottages and farmsteads known as Little Blenheim, Ragnell, Ramsey and Seldom Seen. Ragnell (or Radgnoll, or Radmell) Farm, like Little Blenheim, was demolished in the early 20th century. Ramsey (probably meaning 'island with ramsons') was mentioned in the earlier 13th century and gave its name to a local family mentioned until the early 14th. It was a small collection of fields and meadows bounded, like Noah's Ark, by the river to the south-east and a brook to the north-west.

Ramsey island stretched from Noah's Ark south as far as the site of a later Ramsey Farm, but any settlement there was probably never more than a short-lived farmstead or small group of farmsteads, and there were no buildings by the 18th century. Just south of Northmoor Lock was the site of the later Ramsey Farm, built by 1830 and demolished around 1900. Its associated farm buildings disappeared by the 1950s, although a new house named Church Farm (as distinct from the much older Church Farm House in the village) now stands on almost the same spot as Ramsey farmhouse once did.

Seldom Seen Farm, which still survived in 1930, was just inland from the spot now known as Hart's bridge. Although Robert Florey of Rectory Farm recalls clambering over tumbledown stone walls as a child, these homes are now mostly marked by nothing much more than bare patches in the earth.

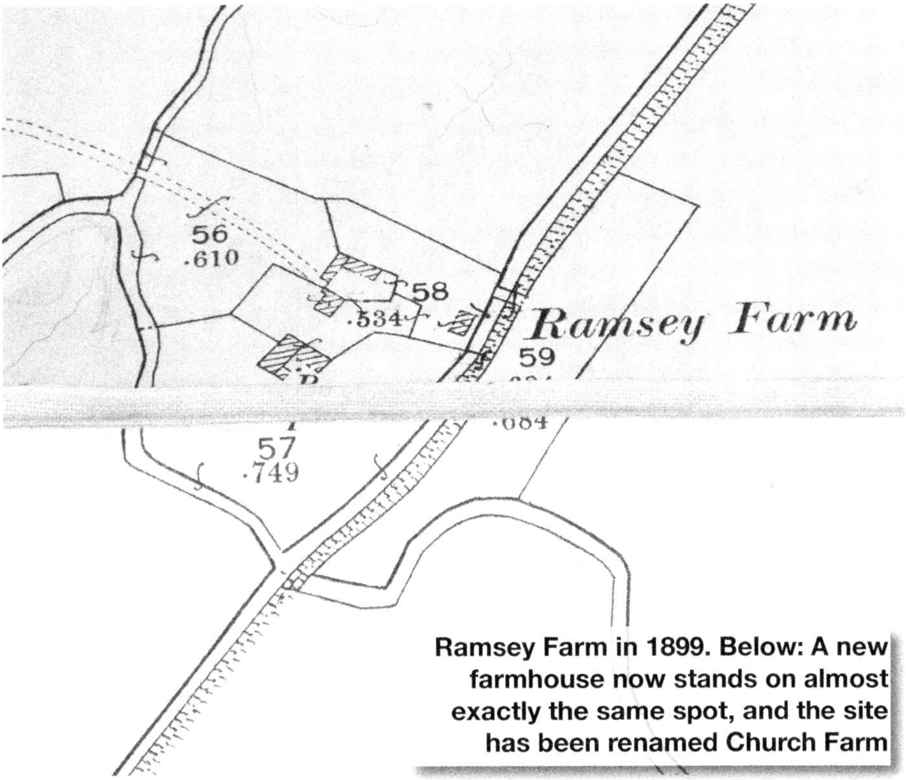

Ramsey Farm in 1899. Below: A new farmhouse now stands on almost exactly the same spot, and the site has been renamed Church Farm

17

A typical paddle and rhymer weir on the Thames, from an engraving in *The Book of the Thames from its Rise to its Fall* (1859) by Mr and Mrs S. C. Hall

In 1763 Noah's Ark island formed the backdrop to a great romance. A student at Christ Church called William Flower came to Noah's Ark weir to enjoy a day's fishing and displayed considerable taste by falling in love with a Northmoor girl. She was Betty Ridge, daughter of the weir-keeper.

Weir-keepers often also provided refreshments, and Betty's father Thomas seems to have been something of a go-getter. Hailing originally from Buckland, he had married his cousin Elizabeth secretly because her parents did not approve of the match. He set his family up in Northmoor, where he served as a member of the vestry committee, and is named in the parish registers of 1745 as 'Thos. Ridge of Noah's Ark: Constable'. Presumably he must have been deemed a respectable member of the community to be allotted the role of enforcing law and order – although a degree of brawn may also have been considered desirable.

Eventually, Thomas gained his victualler's licence, and put his pretty daughter Betty to work plying users of the river with ale. The difficulty was that at the age of nine William Flower had inherited the titles Viscount Ashbrook and Baron Castle Durrow, County Kilkenny. Apparently insensible of their good fortune, William's guardians opposed his choice of viscountess and, as he was only 19, he could not marry without their consent. So while William waited for his twenty-first birthday, he finished his studies at Oxford. At the same time, Betty was

18

Above: Castle Durrow in Ireland, family seat of the Ashbrooks. Below: The house built on Noah's Ark island for the Ridge family by Viscount Ashbrook

Betty Ridge: Northmoor's own Cinderella, a fisher-girl who married a viscount in 1766

Entry from the marriage register for 1766

reported to have been sent away from home to acquire the education and accomplishments appropriate to her new role.

After three years of waiting, on 20th March 1766, William and Betty were married quietly by special licence at St Denys' church. The young couple set up home at Shellingford Manor near Faringdon and, eight months after the wedding, their first child was baptised in Shellingford church. Perhaps even William's patience had its limits. Sadly, William died in 1780 at the age of 36, and Betty was left with six children under the age of 14. The heir was only 13, so Betty found herself responsible for overseeing his interests which included estates in England, Ireland and Wales. But her remarkable Ridge determination came to the fore. As a young widow, she took her son over to Ireland to introduce him to his tenantry and neighbours. Then in 1846, a little over a century on from Betty's own humble birth on an island the river Thames, her granddaughter Charlotte Augusta (right) became Duchess of Marlborough and chatelaine of Blenheim Palace (below) by marrying George Spencer Churchill, sixth Duke of Marlborough.

Never underestimate the women of Northmoor.

● *The Water Gypsy: how a Thames fishergirl became a viscountess* by Julie Ann Godson, ISBN 9781784075545, £10.99

The weirs on this stretch of the Thames were swept away in 1896 and replaced by the Victorian lock between the former Hart's and Ark weirs. Widower Richard Basson was lock-keeper in 1901, and lived here with his elderly father and widowed sister. Mary acted as house-keeper in return for a home for herself and her two young sons, one of whom was born, intriguingly, in Canada.

The Northmoor herd of acclaimed Red Ruby Devon cattle can sometimes be seen helping themelves to a drink from the river bank. Inset: Lambert & Butler cigarette cards from 1907

Church Road
to the old post office

Rectory Farm has been known variously over the years as Glebe Farm and Parsonage Farm and, being immediately south-east of St Denys', its association with the church is clear

THE ROAD THROUGH Northmoor, known as 'Oxford Way' in 1666, formed part of an early route from Abingdon and Oxford through Standlake and on to the wool towns of the Cotswolds. Most of the older houses stand well back from the modern road behind drainage ditches, with a wide belt of what used to be common land in front.

Lower Farm was owned in the 16th and 17th centuries by the yeoman family Fairbeard, and in 2010 parts of the medieval barns were beautifully re-thatched during their conversion to a dwelling now known as Paddock Barn. Watkins Farm was probably named for the family of Charles Watkins, churchwarden and overseer in the late 18th century. Baptism records reveal that Charles Watkins'

Paddock Barn, Lower Farm, 2012

Watkins Farm

Below: Romano-British copper alloy ring found at Watkins Farm during excavations in the 1980s

25

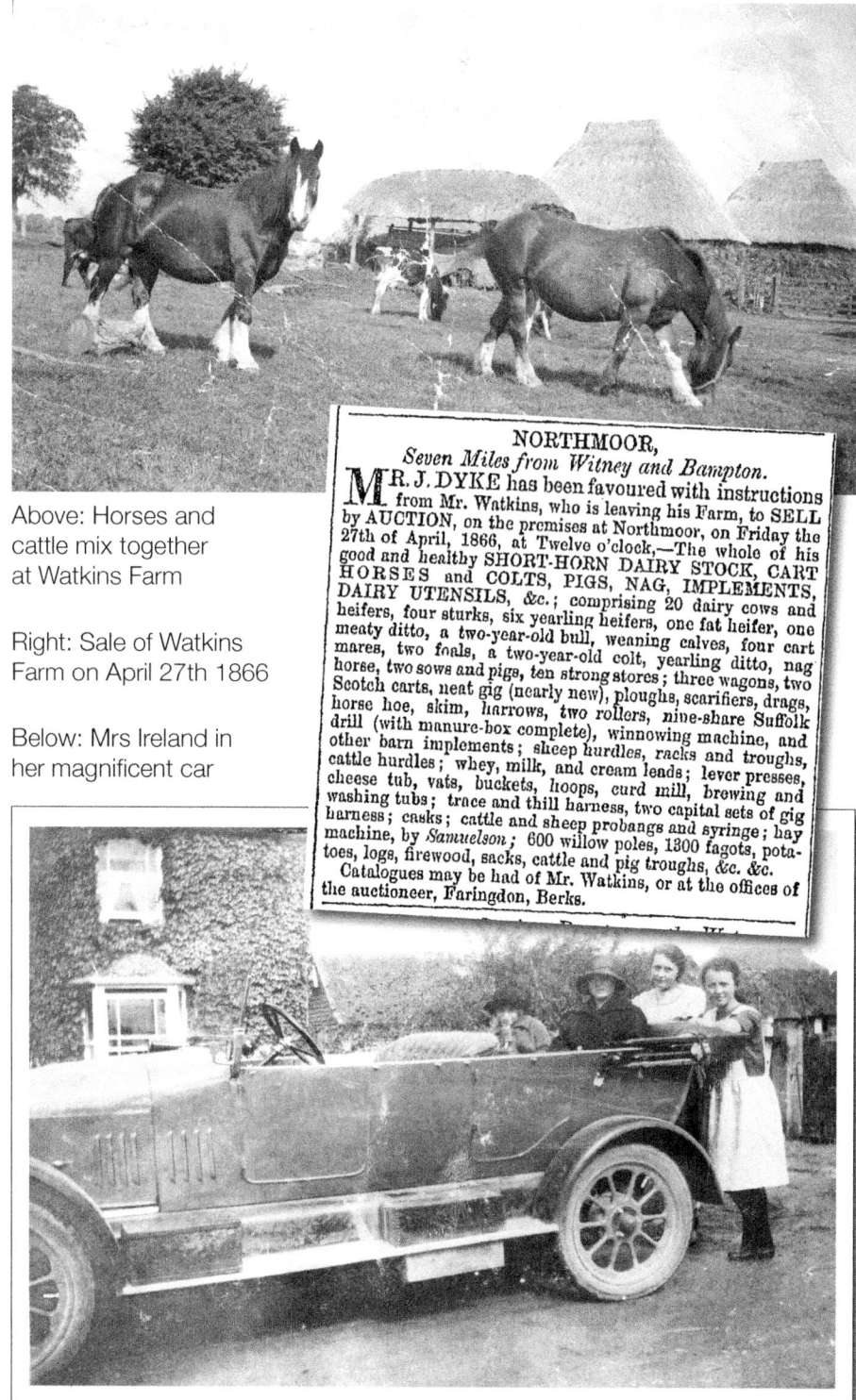

Above: Horses and cattle mix together at Watkins Farm

Right: Sale of Watkins Farm on April 27th 1866

Below: Mrs Ireland in her magnificent car

NORTHMOOR,
Seven Miles from Witney and Bampton.

MR. J. DYKE has been favoured with instructions from Mr. Watkins, who is leaving his Farm, to SELL by AUCTION, on the premises at Northmoor, on Friday the 27th of April, 1866, at Twelve o'clock.—The whole of his good and healthy SHORT-HORN DAIRY STOCK, CART HORSES and COLTS, PIGS, NAG, IMPLEMENTS, DAIRY UTENSILS, &c.; comprising 20 dairy cows and heifers, four sturks, six yearling heifers, one fat heifer, one meaty ditto, a two-year-old bull, weaning calves, four cart mares, two foals, a two-year-old colt, yearling ditto, nag horse, two sows and pigs, ten strong stores; three wagons, two Scotch carts, neat gig (nearly new), ploughs, scarifiers, drags, horse hoe, skim, harrows, two rollers, nine-share Suffolk drill (with manure-box complete), winnowing machine, and other barn implements; sheep hurdles, racks and troughs, cattle hurdles; whey, milk, and cream leads; lever presses, cheese tub, vats, buckets, hoops, curd mill, brewing and washing tubs; trace and thill harness, two capital sets of gig harness; casks; cattle and sheep probangs and syringe; hay machine, by *Samuelson*; 600 willow poles, 1300 fagots, potatoes, logs, firewood, sacks, cattle and pig troughs, &c. &c.

Catalogues may be had of Mr. Watkins, or at the offices of the auctioneer, Faringdon, Berks.

wife Ann presented him with 20 children between 1792 and 1818 – although the repetition of some names suggests that not all made it into adulthood. Perhaps as a result of the wear and tear of such a large family, Watkins farmhouse was substantially rebuilt in the later 19th century. The Irelands were there by 1901 and farmed for many years, retiring eventually to West View, the house they built on the opposite side of the road. From there Elijah drove his trap to Witney market every week with his mother-in-law Amy Smith perched on a dining chair on top.

Right: October 1940. Elijah Ireland driving his mother-in-law to market on a dining chair

Below: West View when newly-built by the Irelands, and (inset) elegantly matured today

Harry Calcutt of Pencots exhibits his no-nonsense approach to pest control as he shows off his neat vegetable patch

Pencots (above), further south, named from 17th- and 18th-century tenants of Northmoor manor, incorporates an earlier 17th-century stone-walled house. Among other references, William Pencot appears in the church registers of the late 17th and early 18th centuries as a man of some substance – churchwarden, parish constable and Poor Law overseer.

During the 19th century, Pencots was divided into a multitude of separate dwellings. A map dated 1876 suggests that the main building alone was split into some six or more homes, and the 1901 census return lists many familiar Northmoor names there, including no less than three Buckingham households, as well as Calcutts, Curtises, Fosters, and Walkers – a community of at least 19 people. Upon the dispersal of the Harcourt estate in 1924, Pencots is described in the sale catalogue as comprising 'five cottages'

On the other side of the road, the name of Causeway Cottage is a reminder that, starting just behind the cottage and running parallel with the main road, is the old causeway, now a footpath, but in ancient times doubtless a valuable protection from spreading river waters. Traces survive of this wide thoroughfare continuing through the yard in front of Rectory Farm, under the ancient dovecote, along the south side of the churchyard and across the field to the west of

Left: This view of Causeway Cottage in 2011 is difficult to reconcile with the photo below which, nevertheless, has 'Causeway Cottage' inscribed on the back. The thatched roof burned off completely in 1940, so perhaps during the rebuilding work a new front door was knocked through where the ground floor window once was, and the old door was blocked up?

The view towards Causeway Cottage in the 1880s, and (below) today

the Red Lion public house (which was formerly the village green), eventually meeting Moreton Lane. There is a theory that this was, in fact, the old main route through the village, the only one above flood level until the present and more direct road was raised up from what may have been originally just a bridle path. Behind Causeway Cottage is Clarke's Farm, currently named Brightside House. This is not to be confused with the 'Clarks' somewhere on the

Standlake Road which served as the manor house until Manor Farm was acquired by the 17th century lords of the manor, the Greenways.

Willow Tree Cottage, on the left in this old postcard (above), is a 16th-century timber-framed house which probably once had an open hall. A row of cottages was built nearby by 1844, possibly that now known as Yew Tree Cottage. This latter served as the village post office for many years.

Ferryman's Farm (above) once served as the rectory – indeed on a map of 1876 it is clearly marked 'Vicarage'. Census records show that in 1891 a well-travelled vicar and his family lived here. William Bell, aged 56, is listed as having been born in the East Indies (the area embracing Borneo, Sumatra and Java), as is his 23-year-old daughter Ethel. William's 49-year-old wife Mary was born in Dover, and their housemaid 18-year-old Eliza Withyman hailed from Corfe, Somerset.

Rectory Farm was first mentioned in the records in the 14th century, though the existing house seems to have been built around 1629 on a site probably a little way to the south of its predecessor, since the older gatehouse is not aligned on it. The remains of a moat are visible to the east of the garden and an ancient granary stands near the house. In 1555 the rectory estate was appropriated to St John's College, and over the years further parcels of land were added. The farm was sold to the tenant Mr Patrick Florey in 1970, and at the time of writing four generations of Floreys have farmed in the village.

At the same time that the Bell family was living over at Ferryman's Farm, 'Parsonage Farm' was occupied by Richard Eagle and his two sisters, Jane and Mary. By the age of 32, Eagle was already a prominent local farmer who by the 1880s also held Manor and Moreton Farms, besides freehold land and other farms in Stanton Harcourt and Standlake. They are probably his initials inscribed into the wall of the cottages at the bottom of Chapel Lane.

The pictures above show how Rectory Farm has been admirably preserved. Even the flight of steps shown on the right of the postcard, dated 1916, was reinstated in 2011 using the pile of stones in the foreground of the modern photo.

The farmyard was transferred to Moreton Lane in 2007 (just in time for the floods), and the old yard and barns next to the road were

33

developed at the same time. These changes enabled a programme of careful restoration to the medieval dovecote and granary, and work on the granary in particular brought national acclaim when it was short-listed for a design award by the Royal Institute of British Architects.

The lower part of Rectory Farm's cruck-framed gatehouse is medieval, the upper part having been converted into a pigeon house or dovecote later on. The presence of a pigeon house supports the suggestion of a Benedictine connection with the church: monks were forbidden to eat strong meat but were occasionally permitted to eat pigeon pie. The stables were converted for domestic use in 1987, the thatched roof being destroyed by fire in 2000.

Right: Tom and Nellie Florey came to Rectory Farm in 1915. Here they are pictured at Fairacres, which they built for their retirement in 1960. Their descendants still work Rectory Farm today

Below: The award-winning granary restoration project

Above: The restored dovecote and barn today, the cart (seen below) having been replaced by a 21st-century workhorse

Above: Oops. The thatched roof on the converted barn was destroyed by fire in 2000

Above: In 2008 Walnut House replaced barns to the east of the entrance to Rectory Farm

Left: Four-footed residents still take precedence over vehicles

In 2008 the farmyard at Rectory Farm was moved to a new site on Moreton Lane. The biggest barn on the old site was converted into a dwelling named Rectory Farm Barn

© Steve Good

37

The Church of St Denys at Northmoor seems to have been built in about 1150 but, except for the cylindrical font with its carved sprig of stylised leaves, nothing survives from the 12th-century church. The almost-total rebuilding may have begun with the chancel around 1300 and finished when the north and south

21st December 1872   16th April 1887

CONCERT.—An amateur concert took place in the school room of this parish on Tuesday the 10th inst. in aid of the fund for the restoration of the beautiful old Church of St. Denys. The performers were the Misses Walter and Norie, of Northmoor; Miss Bunyon, of Clifton; the Rev. W. J. Priest, Mus. Bac., Tutor of Magdalen College, Oxford; Dr. Atkinson, of Bampton; Mr. G. Norie, Mr. Pinnock, and some members of the Fyfield Choir. The programme was an excellent one, and the manner in which it was rendered was highly appreciated by a large and enthusiastic audience. The ringers, in honour of the event, rang a merry peal.

NORTHMOOR.

THANKSGIVING SERVICE.—On Tuesday a thanksgiving service was held in Northmoor Church to commemorate the completion of the work of restoration. Evensong commenced at three o'clock, the Church being crowded. An eloquent discourse was delivered by the Rev. Dr. Bellamy, President of St. John's College and the Vice-Chancellor of Oxford University. The collection, which was for the purchase of a new harmonium, amounted to 12l. 2s. The parish is greatly indebted to the Rev. M. and Mrs. Meyrick for the great interest they have taken in the restoration. The Church has been re-seated with open seats, the walls have been scraped, the chancel repaired by St. John's College, and the floor re-laid with wood blocks.

39

14th-century effigies in the north transept of a knight and a lady, probably Sir Thomas de la More (fl. 1330x1357) and his wife Isabel

The Norman font: the only survival from the original 12th-century church

The porch on the south side shows that the church was built to face the old path through the dovecote

transepts were completed in the mid-14th century, courtesy of the de la More family.

The de la More family was associated with the church from its earliest days. John of More is recorded as rector in 1229, and Thomas More was, intriguingly, ejected from the post in 1418. The final representative of the More family in the post, the Reverend William Moore, died at Rectory Farm in 1612 having served as Northmoor's vicar for an impressive 53 years.

Other notable incumbents were Richard of Chaddesley (1312–15) who later served as a royal envoy, and William Cogyn (c.1439), said to be 'of noble race', who was chaplain to Richard Beauchamp, earl of Warwick. John Haile (1530), even though he had by then moved on from Northmoor, must have caused a ripple of interest back in the village by being hanged at Tyburn on 4th May 1535, presumably for refusing to acknowledge Henry VIII as supreme head of the church of England. On the plus side for Haile, he was eventually beatified by the Pope in 1886. Another turbulent priest was Leonard Stopes who was sacked almost as soon as he arrived in 1559. Catholic tendencies again seem to have been the problem, since Stopes later died in prison as a Catholic missionary priest. Northmoor's first female vicar and present incumbent, Reverend Sarah Sharp, was appointed in 2003.

The 15th-century tower is the most recent part of the main building. A south porch was added in the 16th or 17th century, suggesting that the main thoroughfare through the village was at that time to the south of the church, not to the north as it is now. A less welcome modification came in the form of bullet holes in the tower's north buttress, inflicted as a result of Royalist target practice during the Civil War. Traces of wall paintings in the north transept suggest that it –and maybe the entire church – was once richly-decorated.

Left: Medieval corbel

The lavishly-carved 17th-century altar rail was until 1843 in St John's College chapel

VICARS, RECTORS & CURATES OF ST DENYS', NORTHMOOR

1229	John de Mora	1534	Robert Woodward
1239	Thomas Gaylhun	1535	William ?
1270	William de Clifford	1544-63	John Warner
To 1294	Hugh de Clifford	1554-59	John Peirson
1293	William de Dunaneneye	1559	Leonard Stopes
1294	R. William	1559-1612	William Moore
1296-1311	Sir R. Valentine de Tangeley	1612	John Soane
1312	Richard de Chaddeslegh	1631-35	John Lufton
1315	Robert de Piriton	1635	? Rumble
1343	Stephen de la More	1641	Thomas Miles
1347	John Corbet	1644	Edmund Tillesley
1347	Robert de Mildenhale	1664	Clifton Stone
1351	William de Burgh	?-1668	John Brasier
1353	John Costre	1668	George Merryfield
1356	William de Aldebury	1676-82	Henry Davies
To 1373	Matthew atte Yate	1681-4	Edward Waple
1373	Richard de Herbergh	1682-88/9	Richard Maris
1377	Nicholas Moryn	1684	Ambrose Bonwicke
1378	Geoffrey de la Roche	1688	Arthur Buckeridge
1394	William Lincoln	1690-6	John Stileman
By 1394	John Pernot	1696	George Pickerne
1395-1406	Henry de Corbrigg	1704	Samuel Smith
1418	Thomas More	1706-8	John Pridie
1418	Henry de Clayton	1709	Moses Wyles
By 1432	Walter Pursthorp	1712	William Bridge
By 1439	William Cogeyn	1716, 1722	Thomas Heywood
1465-1501	Richard Bird	1728	Winch Holdsworth
1517	?	1734	William Walker
?	John Taylor	1737	James Luck
By 1526	Robert Welsshe	1746	James Musgrave
	Christopher Hylle	-1755	Edward Berdmore
By 1530-35	John Hale	1755-8	John Saunders

VICARS, RECTORS & CURATES OF ST DENYS', NORTHMOOR

1758	Ashton Thorpe	1832-3	Henry Bristow Wilson
-1769	John Cheshire Heyborne	1834-5	Lancelot Arthur Sharpe
1764-90	William Seward	1835-8	Thomas Chandler Curties
1769-70	Thomas Clare	1839-43	Arthur Philip Dunlap
1770	Samuel Dennis	1843-55	Henry Heming
1772	Richard Dickson Shackleford	1855-8	Arthur Brydon Cross Starkey
-1774	Nathaniel Moore	1858-67	Edward Coupland
1774-5	William Finch	1867-71	Edward Beachcroft Devon
1775	John Cobb	1872	John Charles Coen
1776-8	John Mitchell	1875-76	Henry E. Wardroper
1778-9	George Piggott	1879-80	William Henry Penney
1779-82	Richard Dickson Shackleford	1881-85	Lewis Stacey Tuckwell
1782-5	John Applebee	1886	Maurice Meyrick
1785	John Green	1891-1901	William Charles Bell
1786	Elias Benjamin de la Fountaine	1901	John Reginald George
1788-90	William Finch	1911	J.E. Cardigan Williams
1790-4	George Francis Blakiston		I.I. Turner
1794-5	James Cutler	1915	Alfred Griffiths
1795	Jonathan Gardner	1925	R.S. Edwards
1795-6	William Musgrave	1927	John Hilton Stowell
1797-1801	Edward Drax Free	1934	Cedric William Farrer
1801-33	Thomas Birch	1954	Herbert Cutler
1802-4	James Saunders	1959	Arthur Sherwood Caswell
1804-10	William Wise	1970	W. John Fletcher-Campbell
1810-15	Thomas Speidell	1975	Michael Farthing
1815-19	James Matthews	1983	James McCloghry
1819-23/2	Thomas Silver	1990	Paul Cadogan
1823-27	George Gleed	1995	David Murray
1826	Philip Wynter	2003-13	Sarah Sharp
-1827	John Gutch	2014	Andrew Tweedy
1827-8	Henry Payne		
1829-32	Edward Parris New		*Compiled by Henry Herford*

Medieval corbel, church of St Denys

Postmaster George Baston

© Oxfordshire County Council – Oxfordshire History Centre

A postal service through Witney existed by the 1850s but, until at least 1876, Northmoor had no post office of its own – the nearest one was in Eynsham. However, George Baston (above right) was described as 'postmaster' in the parish register at the baptism of his son Walter in 1889. Mr Baston ran his post office from Church Cottage (above), and Kelly's Directory for 1891 reveals that letters arrived from Oxford via Eynsham at 9.15 am, and were dispatched at 5.10 pm. He was still there in 1901, but by 1908 Mrs Baston was running the post office on her own.

The post office moved to Chapel Lane, and eventually closed down in the late 1960s.

Reg Berry and the Cherries

Much missed: Former resident Chris Blakey (right), the Venturers' original leader

Northmoor's architect-designed village hall replaced an older, timber-built one north of the pub in the mid-1990s. With its high, arched ceiling and maple floor, the hall has served as the venue for a wide range of community activities since 1997. Every week the Thursday Club provides a hot lunch and entertainment for the elderly of the area plus their carers, and on a Tuesday evening the village band Reg Berry and the Cherries gets together in the hall for rehearsals. A monthly village market offers shoppers an opportunity to buy locally-produced food and crafts while enjoying a chat with neighbours over tea and cakes, and the annual Christmas market gives us all a head start on our Christmas shopping while at the same time raising funds for a different charity each year.

The Northmoor Venturers, founded by Chris Blakey in 2013, continues to organise activities for the village's younger residents, with an emphasis on acquiring social skills, self-confidence and an awareness of responsibility towards others.

The Northmoor Players is our award-winning amateur dramatic society, renowned for the professional quality of their pantomimes which are staged in early February every other year or so. In 2012 the Players won first prize in the Oxford Drama Network Pantomime Competition for their production of *Treasure Island: the panto* (above), no mean feat for such a small village.

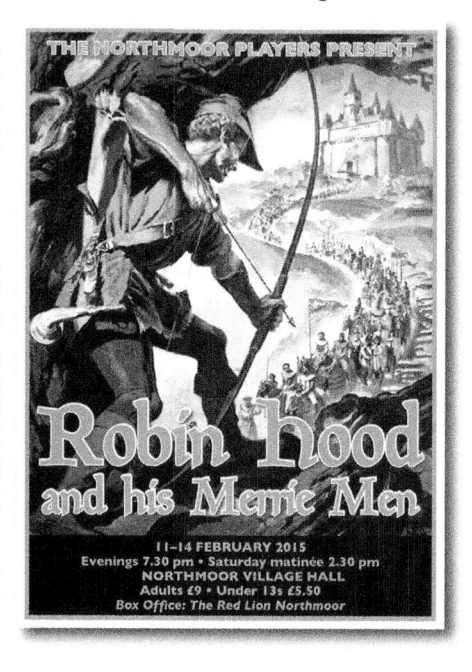

The Northmoor Quilt was stitched through the summer and autumn of 2014.
Back: Carrie Berry, Jean Lamb, Gai Coleman, Caroline Wheatley, Lisa Ellett, Amy Paterson, Mary Anne Florey, Andrea Freeman. Front: Elizabeth Druce, Lindsay Herford, Kim Fowler, Naomi Owen, Julie Thorne, Julie Williams

Since 2012 the Northmoor Flower and Produce Show has been organised annually by Maureen Sears. Classes for vegetables, fruit and flowers are shown alongside savoury and sweet baking, preserves, art, photography and crafts. Children aged 16 and under have their own classes, and entrants from the surrounding villages are always welcome.

51

Northmoor School

A game of Ring o' Roses in the school playground in the 1970s. The children are (left to right): James Druce, Christine Rankin(?), Julian Wade, Steven Horne, Caroline Wade, Rachel Wilce. The barns in the background were replaced by Walnut House in 2008

IN THE EARLIER 17th century the children of Northmoor were given a degree of education, presumably of a religious nature, in the church. By 1841 the census listed Mrs Sophia Robin as 'schoolmistress'; Mrs Robin perhaps succeeded Ursula Morris in the role. Poor Mrs Morris does not appear to have profited greatly by the profession – in 1851 she was described as 'Pauper, formerly Schoolmistress' and had been obliged to move in with her daughter and son-in-law. Mary Ann Bennett was serving as schoolmistress in 1871, assisted by her 67-year-old mother.

A National (i.e. Church of England) School was opened in 1873 in a new, stone-and-slated schoolroom on former church land. The register rose from 32 to 53 within a year, though in 1876 over half the pupils were from a short-lived orphanage in Northmoor where children were trained to enter useful occupations.

National Schools were gradually absorbed into the state system, and in 1881 local girl Rachel Gardner was assistant to Jane Husslington from Lancashire. Perhaps the intractable children of Northmoor were a bit too much for these ladies, because inspectors' reports were often critical, and in 1890 things had reached such a pass that the lord of the manor, Edward William Harcourt of Nuneham Park, actually withheld his annual subscription. By 1891 Miss Husslington was gone, replaced by Sarah King and

Right: An early 20th-century silver pocket watch inscribed 'To William Webb for good conduct and attendance'. The watches were made for Oxfordshire Education Committee by Rowells of Oxford

her assistant. But, whereas Rachel Gardner had lived at home with her mother, Miss King's assistant lives in the school house.

By 1901 Hannah Viggers had arrived mob-handed from Essex. Mrs Viggers was equipped with no fewer than two assistants with which to marshal the flower of Northmoor youth. Along with her sister Elinor and her own daughter Gertrude, Mrs Viggers oversaw the addition of a new classroom in 1902 in order to meet government requirements.

It is somehow unsurprising to learn that by 1904 the school was described as being 'admirably conducted', and by 1907 the register had risen to 47. The youth of Northmoor was not about to take this sort of thing lying down, however, and by 1919 a fresh generation of children appears to be renewing the attack. The school was acknowledged to have 'special difficulty', and pupils were often aspiring only to the level of 'backward'.

Senior pupils were moved to Standlake from 1929, when 11 children were transferred, leaving 28 infants and juniors at Northmoor. Evacuees from Stangate, south London, accompanied by their two teachers, swelled the roll to 38 in 1940, but the departure of the incomers meant that the number plummeted to just 12 in 1945. In 1957 the school was forced to down-size to a single class and several children were transferred elsewhere, but by 1971 the roll rallied to 26. Those who grew up in the village at that time will remember Mrs Walker, headmistress for almost 20 years, and her assistant Mrs Farren. The school closed in 1981, and the children were transferred to Standlake.

55

1935

1955

1936

196?

1938

196?

1939

196?

57

Chapel Lane

The pair of brick-built cottages at the southern end of Chapel Lane bear the inscription 'R.E 1873', a reference to the probable builder, farmer Richard Eagle. They remain very little changed to this day

A GATE ON the northern side of the main road through Northmoor opens onto a farm track which runs up through a ford. A map of 1843 suggests that Dag Lane, mentioned from the 15th century and the predecessor of Chapel Lane, ran north-westwards from the area between this gate and the entrance to Hollyhock and Virginia Cottages, through the ford, and then behind the modern allotments, parallel with the more recent lane.

In 1929 the Reverend J. H. Stowell reported that his enquiries suggested a 'dag' was a kind of barrow with four wheels and no sides. Legend had it at that time that, when a girl from Dag Lane came to church to be married, she was brought on a dag or wheelbarrow, which would certainly make sense if she had to traverse a ford in her wedding finery. However, other sources suggest that a dag was either a small dagger or even an early type of pistol. In any event, Dag Lane is a name still in use in a strip of counties running up the centre of England, from Oxfordshire to Buckinghamshire and on up into Northamptonshire, Leicestershire and Derbyshire.

Whilst the modern footpath running north from the main road now joins this older track for a few metres only before swerving abruptly through the allotments to join onto the newer lane, the 1843 map suggests that Dag Lane continued roughly north, passing between Chapel Row and Old Farm Cottage, and then terminating at what is now the back of Greystones, but which must once have been the front of the cottages facing the lane.

During the 20th century a post office was run by Mrs Bint from number 2, presently known as 'Fireflies'. It closed in the 1960s c.1970: The row of trees between Chapel Row (with thatch) and Old Farm Cottage reveals the route of Chapel Lane's predecessor, Dag Lane

Thus Dag Lane formed part of an ancient thoroughfare which can still be traced on the map today, running north-west past Linch Hill in the direction of Witney. South of our main road, a field boundary behind the old Clarks Farm runs down to the river crossing near Northmoor Lock, then a farm track runs into Appleton and the route proceeds through the north-east corner of Tubney Wood to Gozzard's Ford and on to Abingdon.

A map of Northmoor dated 1843 shows that Chapel Lane did not exist at that date, but a bridleway began opposite the church and ran along the south-eastern boundary of Church (or West) field, and then turned parallel but slightly to the west of the older Dag Lane at its northern end.

In that same year a brick chapel was built on the east side of the bridleway and next to the track leading to Old Farm Cottage. During the first half of the

19th century the hard-pressed labouring classes felt that their particular concerns were not sufficiently addressed by the Church of England, and Northmoor was not unusual in succumbing to the national craze for Methodism. The parish map of 1899 (opposite, below) shows the little building occupying a corner of what is now the pretty garden at 'Moonwinds'. So it must have been around this time that the bridleway became a 25-foot carriage road extending to the parish's northern boundary and known as Chapel Lane.

Boosted by the non-residence of Northmoor's vicar, the chapel was wildly popular, with a recorded 90 people in the morning congregation on one day in 1851 and 150 in the evening, when on the same day the church could manage only 50 and 60 respectively. It was eventually closed in 1920, and by 1930 it had been demolished.

Parish Cottages, now Greystones, was rebuilt in 1797 by local farmer John Nalder. Greystones is noticeably set back from the lane; this is because what now appears to be the front of the house would once have been the rear of a row known then as Parish Cottages. The present parking area in front of the house was once cottage gardens stretching as far as the bridleway that preceded Chapel Lane. The row was built not to face onto the bridleway, but onto the older Dag Lane which terminated at this point. On the left of the group in the photograph below is George Brooker, who is listed as a 12-year-old agricultural labourer in the 1881 census, making him 32 years old in this picture. He wears the Boer War uniform of the Queen's Own Oxfordshire Hussars ('Queer Objects on Horseback'), dating the photograph to around 1901.

Parish Cottages, currently known as 'Greystones'

While absent from an 1843 map, Mount Pleasant (above) appeared by 1876. Just over a century later, work started to extract gravel from the parish, and the field immediately behind Mount Pleasant was turned into a lake as a result. At the beginning of the 21st century the old house at Mount Pleasant was developed into the thoroughly up-to-date home shown in the photograph below. As elsewhere in the parish, the trend for abandoning former place-names in favour of the cutely rustic continues. Behold: Mount Pleasant has become 'Walnut Cottage'.

Look! No gravel pits!

Who needs pesky old food anyway?

The Red Lion to Cow Lane

Christ Church and New College beagles meet at the Red Lion in the autumn of 1963

THE RED LION in Northmoor stands on the site of the church house. During the medieval period games and entertainments were held in the churchyard after Sunday Mass in order to raise money to maintain the fabric of the church. Eventually it was decided that the churchyard was not an appropriate place for the brawling and drunkenness that often resulted, and separate buildings known as 'church houses' were constructed nearby in order to contain any unseemly behaviour.

The church house in Northmoor was rebuilt around 1741, and opened as an inn probably in the 1770s. The inn also contained a grocer's shop by 1861, and the proprietor in 1891 is listed as Edwin James Hutt. The village stocks stood near the Red Lion in the mid 18th century, presumably on the village green which was sited on what is now a field to the west of the Red Lion.

Right: The Red Lion, community pub. Below: A postcard dated 31st December 1905

Above: Landlord Lew Brain and a friend put out the bunting at the end of World War II, while Bonzo the dog departs on a mission. And (below) a rather less successful campaign: flags supporting England's World Cup football team in the summer of 2010. Opposite, top: Lew Brain and his daughter Hazel in the cellar in the 1950s. Seen alongside the drinks are some of the groceries also available to patrons

Lew Brain and his daughter Hazel

Following a community buy-out in 2014, the pub is now run by the award-winning Ian and Lisa Neale

LANDLORDS OF THE RED LION

1800-23	Richard Clack
1837-54	Thomas Walter
1861	John Cooling
1864-68	John Cripps
1869-83	James Walker
1887	William Walker
1891	Edwin James Hutt
1899	James Hutt
1901	Arthur William Hutt
1903	Jane Hutt
1907-15	George Walker
1924-28	Frederick Butler
1931-37	Frederick Timms
1937-66	Lewis G Brain
1966-68	Raymond Cooper
1968-72	Alistair Fogg
1972-89	Roy Fuller
1989-94	Chris Hitchens
1994-2008	John Emery
2008-13	Colin Belland
2014	Ian & Lisa Neale

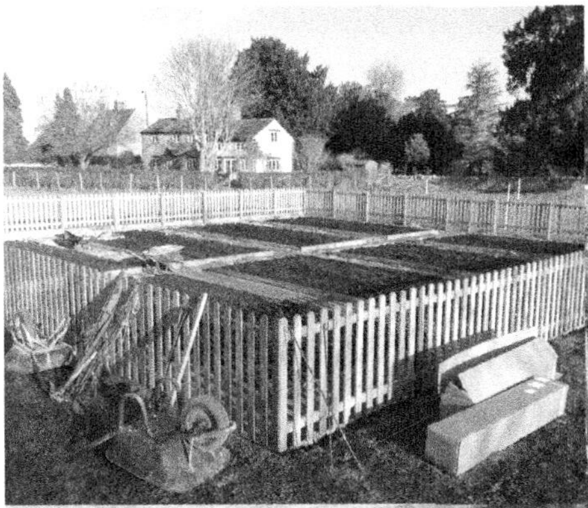
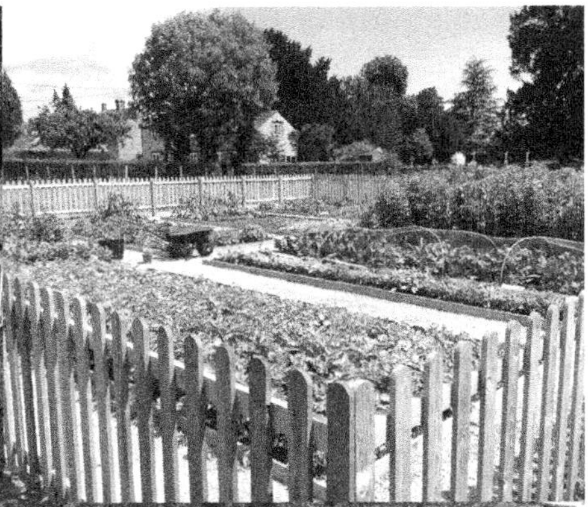
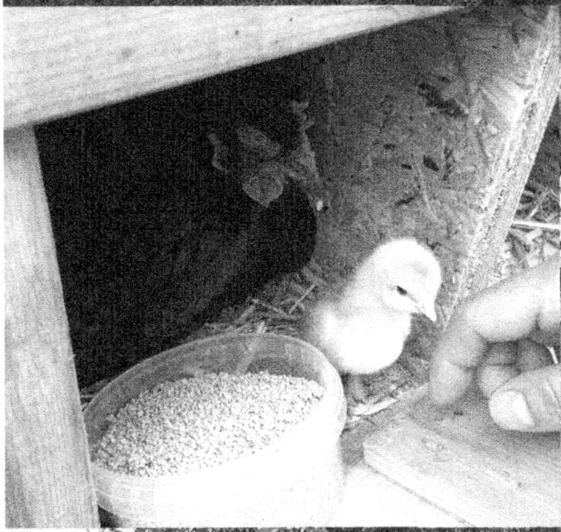
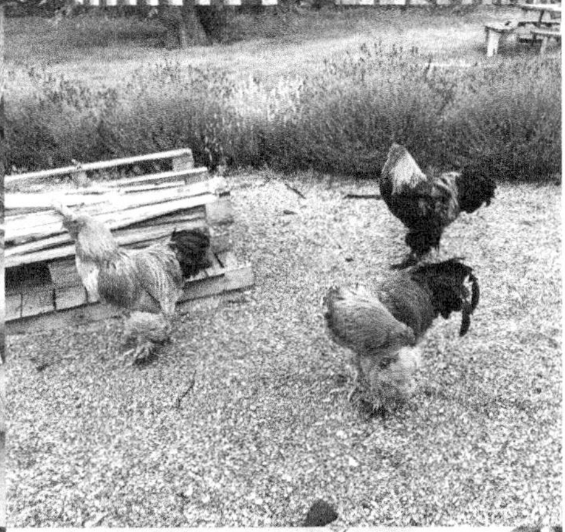
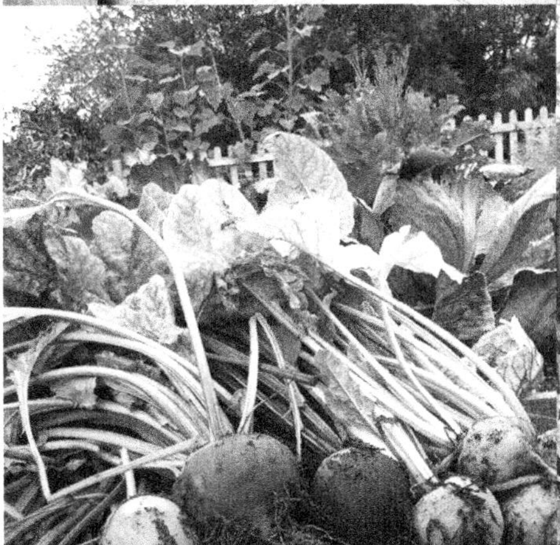
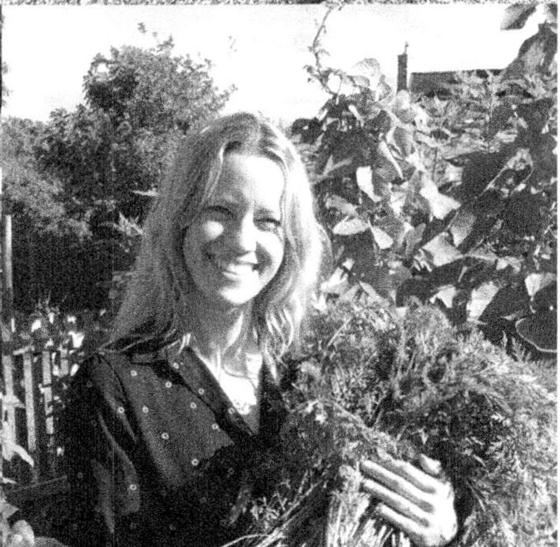

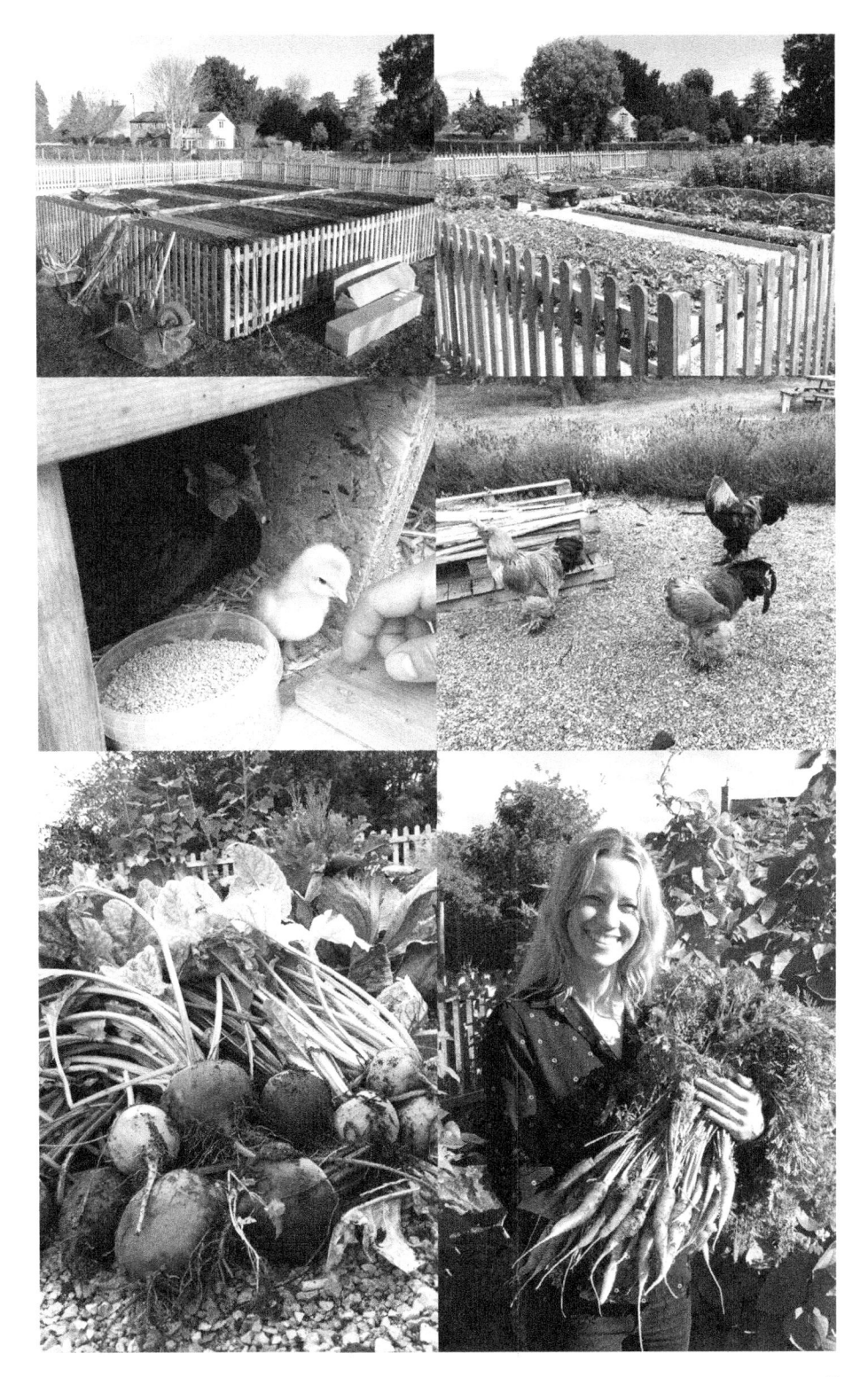

To the south of the old green is Church Farm House, an 18th-century house with an almost square main block, which was remodelled in the later 19th century. Perhaps then the central stack was reconstructed with a passage between the formerly back-to-back fireplaces. A short kitchen wing at the rear, perhaps part of an earlier house, retains a possibly re-used fireplace beam with the date 1679 and the initials probably of Thomas and Katherine Martin, implying that this was the chief house of the Martins' large freehold before its sale to the Harcourts in 1719.

Opposite the old village green stands a thatched terrace known as Red Lion Cottages, probably built by local farmer John Nalder in the 18th century. In 1892–23 a vicarage, designed by John Oldrid Scott, was built on land behind these cottages. It was sold around 1960 to raise funds for a new vicarage at Stanton Harcourt to serve the united benefice.

A 1920s postcard showing the brick and timber construction of Red Lion Cottages. The materials may have been brought from Noah's Ark. The stamp has gone, but the postcard is sent from '15 Northmoor'

Red Lion Cottages: autumn 1969

Below: Mrs Cantwell, mother of Norman (left) and his sister Maggie, and wife to Fred Cantwell, stands at the front door of number 3 in the 1930s

The cottage on the corner of Baker's Lane, pictured here in 2011, houses large ovens

NORTHMOOR, NEAR ENSHAM.   1837
Household Furniture, Shop Goods, and Effects.
TO BE SOLD BY AUCTION,
By Mr. LONG,
On the premises at Northmoor, on Friday next the 9th of June, to commence at Eleven o'clock,—All the useful HOUSEHOLD FURNITURE, STOCK of GROCERY, BREAD and FLOUR, SHOP FIXTURES, and other Property of Mr. Wheeler, baker and shopkeeper.
Catalogues and particulars may be had of the auctioneer, Witney; and on the premises.

In 1892-3 a new vicarage, designed by John Oldrid Scott, was built on land provided by the Harcourt estate. It was sold c.1960 to raise funds for a house at Stanton Harcourt to serve the united benefice

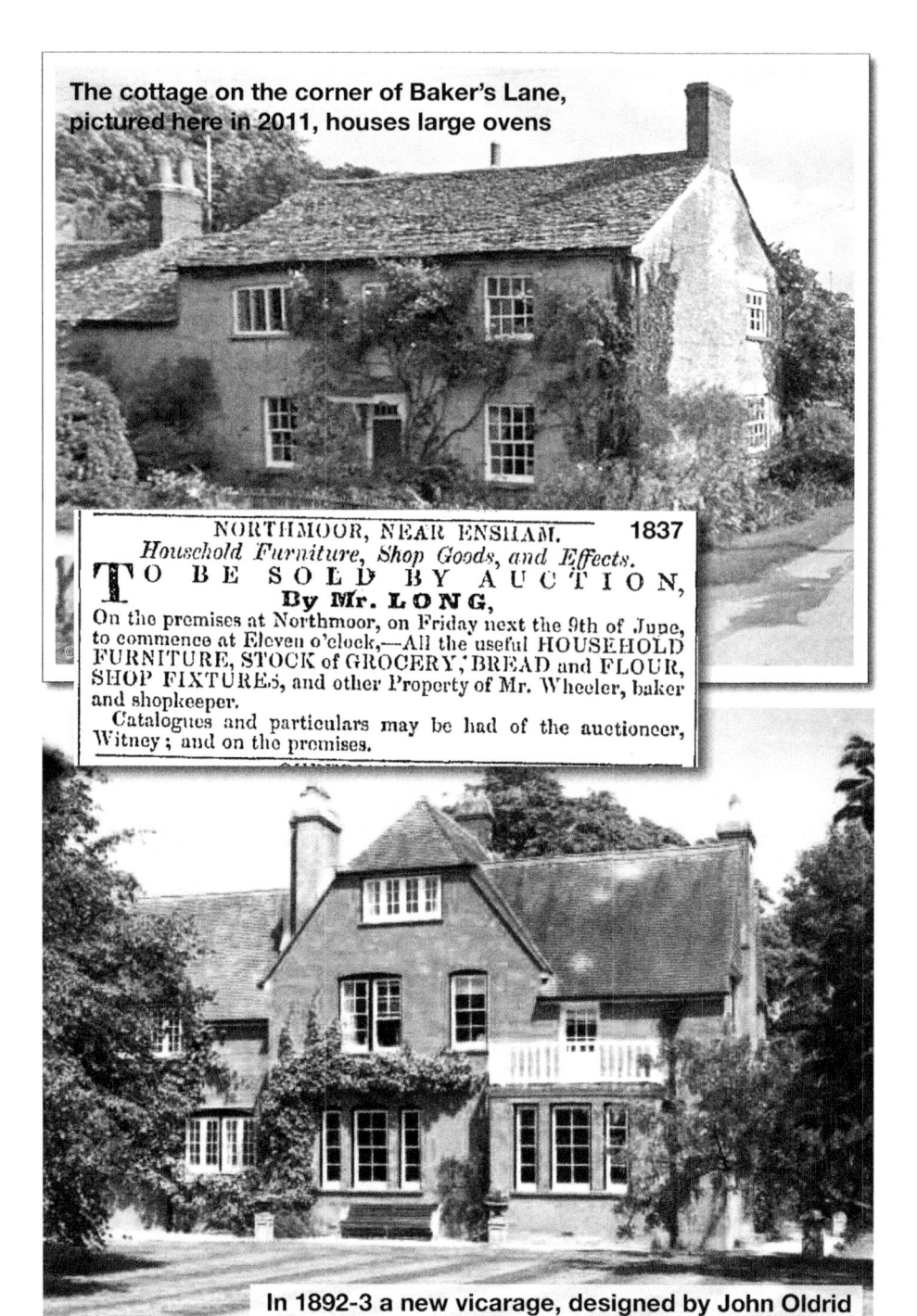

The Dun Cow Inn, now a private home, opened around 1793 and was re-built c.1800 and, like the Red Lion, also housed a shop by 1861. In *Kelly's Directory* of 1891 the publican is named as Moses Buckingham, and in 1901 George Butler has taken over. The pub closed in 1990.

THE DUN COW, NORTHMOOR,
About 6 miles from Oxford, and the same distance from Witney.
SALE UNDER A DISTRESS FOR RENT.
Mr. JOHN B. KING
WILL SELL BY AUCTION, on the premises, as above, on Thursday next, the 9th of January, 1879, at 10 for 11 o'clock punctually.—The useful HOUSEHOLD FURNITURE, STOCK-IN-TRADE, and OUTDOOR EFFECTS; comprising mahogany tables, Windsor chairs, sofas, easy chairs, Singer sewing machine, dinner service, lamps, cases of stuffed birds, excellent suite of bed room furniture, feather beds, blankets, Arabian bedsteads, chests of drawers, kitchen utensils, stock-in-trade of the grocer's shop, quantity of tea, biscuits, sugar, black currant wine, cider, &c. Also a useful brown horse, poultry, rick of hay, quantity of straw and chaff, iron plough, winnowing machine, harness, and sundry other articles, as enumerated in catalogues.—On view the morning of sale. Catalogues at the place of sale; Roebuck Hotel, Oxford; Marlboro' Arms and Fleece Hotels, Witney; Bull Inn, Standlake; and of the auctioneer, High-street, Abingdon.

Above: Joyce Douglas at the Dun Cow during the 1970s, with Len Akers (back) and Fred Rose. Right: Jim Godfrey from Standlake (left) enjoys a pint with David King (centre) and John Lay (right) in 1971

Brook Farm might be used to argue that, in some ways, Northmoor is currently enjoying its salad days. It is hard to believe that the tenants of this now-immaculate property, members of the prominent Walter family, were granted rent reductions during the 1880s as the agricultural depression and poor harvests took their toll. Farmers all over Britain and Ireland had to reduce their prices in the face of grain imports from America and meat from New Zealand and Argentina. By 1891, The Brook is being farmed by Charles Burdon, a single man from Chadlington, then in 1901 John Alexander is there, along with his wife and two small sons.

Stylish Black Poplars was commissioned from Oxford Architectural Design by David Anderson, owner of Brook Farm at the time.

Black Poplars. Inset: Brook Farm in 1928

The Foster family at The Patch c.1903

In 1901 The Patch, now a substantial executive home, was the cottage of agricultural labourer Joseph Foster, his wife Ada, and their three daughters, Elsie, Lilian and Amelia (above). The Patch was used as the gamekeeper's cottage in the 1920s when it was purchased for £80 from the Harcourt estate by Patrick Florey's grandmother, great grandmother to the present farmer at Rectory Farm.

Right: Mr and Mrs Breckon at The Patch c.1970. Below: By the 1980s the thatch is gone, as are the old windows. Below right: Executive home

Lords of the Manor of More

After the dissolution of the monasteries Henry VIII granted the manor to a royal equerry, _John Herle_, who sold it to Queen Elizabeth I's physician _Walter Bayley_ in 1590. Bayley's son sold it some time after 1600 to _James Stone_, and by 1619 it passed to _Henry Greenway_. Greenway's son sold it to _Edward Twyford_ of London, who in turn sold it to _Edmund Warcupp_. Warcupp's daughter Anna Maria sold it in 1718 to _John Blewitt_. Trustees under Blewitt's will sold the manor to the _Harcourt_ family.

Pinnocks Farm was acquired from the trustees of Richard Eagle by Magdalen College at the turn of the 20th century. The farm has been occupied by the same family, the Reeves, since 1936 when the present occupant Grenville's parents came from Wales as tenants.

On the western edge of the parish is Manor Farm, owned by the de la More family from the 13th through to the early 17th century, when the estate was sold off piecemeal. But Manor Farm should not be confused with the manor of Northmoor. In fact, in the early 17th century there seems to have been no manor house for the village. Manor (or More) Farm had been sold to a Mr John Every of Somerset who left it to his son Simon, 1st Baronet Every of Eggington in Derbyshire. (Intriguingly, two centuries on, one of Betty Ridge's granddaughters, Caroline, would marry the son of the 9th Baronet, and her son would become Sir Henry Flower Every, 10th Baronet.)

The lord of the manor at that time, Henry Greenway, is recorded as living in a freehold farmhouse called Clarks on the Standlake Road. Manor Farm, which Greenway purchased from Sir Simon, was once more adopted as the lord's residence by Greenway's son after Henry's death in 1640. Thereafter successive lords of 'More St Dennis' once more occupied the house from 1640 to after 1730, including the Warcupp family who were lords of the manor from 1671 to 1718. A barn at Manor Farm bears the initials and date 'E. W. 1672' – evidence of local notable Sir Edmund Warcupp. Although a captain in the Parliamentary forces in the Civil War, Warcupp later joined General Monck in helping to restore King Charles II to the throne in 1660. He was knighted at Whitehall Palace in December 1684. Manor Farm is the only part of the manor of More still retained by the Harcourt family, and is currently let to tenants.

By direction of the Trustees of the Right Hon. Viscount Harcourt.

OXFORDSHIRE

Within five miles of the City of Oxford, three miles of Witney, and almost adjoining Eynsham and South Leigh Stations.

Particulars, Plans and Conditions of Sale

OF THE

STANTON HARCOURT AND NORTHMOOR PORTIONS OF

The Harcourt Settled Estates

Covering an Area of about

3,363 Acres

COMPRISING ABOUT

Twenty First-class Farms, Small Holdings, Three Free Licensed Houses, Fishing Boxes, Small Residences, and

The Villages of Stanton Harcourt, Northmoor, Sutton and West End, with Long Frontages to the Rivers Thames and Windrush.

WHICH MESSRS.

NICHOLAS

Will Sell by Public Auction,

At the CORN EXCHANGE, OXFORD,

On WEDNESDAY, the 3rd day of SEPTEMBER, 1924,

At 2.30 p.m. precisely.

Copies of these Particulars, Plans and Conditions of Sale may be had of *The Estate Agent*, Mr. HARRY GALE, The Estate Office, Nuneham Courtenay, near Oxford; *The Solicitors*, Messrs. WALKER, MARTINEAU & CO., 36, Theobald's Road, London, W.C.1; or of *The Auctioneers*,

Messrs. NICHOLAS, 4, Albany Court Yard, Piccadilly, W.1; and at Reading, Berks, and Kenton, Middlesex.

Harcourt Settled Estates.

SCHEDULE OF LOTS.

Lot No.	Description.	A.	R.	P.	£	s.	d.
1	Southleigh Ground	11	1	32	18	0	0
2	Tar Wood Lodge	2	2	38	In Hand		
3	Tar Wood	90	1	31			
4	Tar Farm	374	3	19	400	0	0
5	Tar Barn Farm and Tar Wood Farm ...	183	1	4	{ 87	0	0
					63	10	0
6	Beard Mill	109	1	27	176	10	0
7	Part Blackditch Farm and Cottage No. 35	70	3	22	78	6	9
8	Blackditch	191	0	38	203	12	6
9	Sutton Farm	399	3	36	456	10	0
10	Nicholl's Farm	3	3	15	7	10	0
11	Accommodation Pasture	2	0	0	4	0	0
12	Cox's Farm	64	1	4	71	10	0
13	Pinkhill Farm	241	3	38	320	0	0
14	Tawney's Farm	137	0	12	142	16	0
15	Pimm's Farm	146	1	12	170	0	0
16	Cottages Nos. 36 and 37	0	0	26	6	3	4
17	Cottages Nos. 31 and 32, Workshops and Land	0	3	3	11	19	11
18	Cottage No. 30 and Hunt's Close ...	1	3	0	10	18	8
19	Cottage No. 27	1	0	20	12	18	0
20	Cottages Nos. 28 and 29	0	1	2	3	1	8
21	Cottage No. 26	0	1	1	10	16	9
22	Cottage No. 25	0	1	10	5	18	5
23	Cottage No. 22	0	0	32	2	9	10
24	Cottages Nos. 19 and 20	0	1	4	6	2	6
25	"The Harcourt Arms"	2	0	13	23	0	0
26	Cottage No. 54	0	1	15	5	18	4
27	Garden Ground	0	2	23	2	0	0
28	Cottage No. 51	0	0	34	4	10	3
29	Cottage No. 47	0	1	8	4	2	4
30	Cottages Nos. 57, 58 and 59	0	1	6	11	12	6
31	Accommodation Land	5	2	24	10	0	0
32	Cottage No. 46	1	1	1	6	12	8
	Carried forward ...	2,045	2	30	£2,337	10	5

Harcourt Settled Estates.

Schedule of Lots—continued.

Lot No.	Description.	Area. A. R. P.	Rental. £ s. d.
	Brought forward	2,045 2 30	2,337 10 5
33	Cottage No. 45	4 2 9	16 4 9
34	Cottage No. 44	0 2 38	6 8 4
35	Cottage No. 43	0 0 31	2 7 6
36	Cottage No. 42	0 0 35	4 2 4
37	Cottages Nos. 55 and 56	0 0 18	5 18 8
38	Cottage No. 41	0 1 36	4 12 8
39	Cottage No. 40	0 0 30	4 2 4
40	Cottages Nos. 38 and 39	4 3 8	16 4 8
41	West End Farm	165 1 11	200 0 0
42	The Chequers Inn	8 0 15	70 0 0
43	Watkins Farm	228 1 9	285 2 4
44	Pencots (Five Cottages)	0 3 37	18 4 2
45	Clarke's Farm	28 3 10	38 0 0
46	Cottage No. 12	0 0 19	3 11 2
47	Cottage No. 13	0 0 16	1 15 7
48	Cottage No 14	0 0 29	3 11 2
49	Church Farm	217 3 4	265 2 6
50	Moreton Farm	116 1 36	156 0 0
51	Grass and Arable Land	19 3 8	23 10 0
52	Brook Farm	83 1 25	108 0 0
53	The " Rose Revived Inn "	54 0 26	93 0 0
54	Newbridge Mill	69 1 10	89 0 0
55	Manor Farm	204 2 3	250 0 0
56	West Moors	10 2 10	10 0 0
57	Linch Hill, Land	43 0 0	36 0 0
58	Arable Land	55 3 1	42 0 0
	A.	3,363 2 24	£4,090 8 7

Live and Dead Farming Stock,
At Northmoor, near Stanton Harcourt, Oxon.
TO BE SOLD BY AUCTION,
By Mr. T. MALLAM,
On the premises, on Friday the 6th day of November,—The very useful FARMING STOCK, on the Manor Farm at Northmoor, Oxon; consisting of 5 powerful cart horses, valuable 2-year-old cart horse colt, 3-year-old mare ditto, 2 yearling colts, and a nag mare; 33 porkers, and store pigs; 2 good narrow-wheel wagons, useful harness for 6 horses; 2 dung carts, ploughs, harrows, ladders, cow racks, an oak roller, and other useful implements in husbandry.
May be viewed the morning of sale until One o'clock, at which time the auction will commence.
Catalogues may be had at the inns and public-houses in the neighbourhood; place of sale; and of the auctioneer, High-street, Oxford.

1835

1885

NORTHMOOR, NEAR EYNSHAM, OXON.
TO be LET, from the 29th September.—TWO FARMS, situated in the above Parish.
The BROOK FARM, containing about 100 Acres, of which 29 Acres are Pasture, and the remainder very useful Arable; good stock land, with plenty of good water.
The NORTHMOOR FARM, containing about 170 Acres, of which 68 Acres are Pasture, and the remainder Arable; good dairy farm, with a plentiful supply of water.
For particulars apply to Mr. F. Mair, Nuneham Courtenay, Oxford.

Moreton to New Bridge

Seb Boston is accompanied by his Old English Mastiff on a frosty morning in Moreton Lane during December 1962

MORETON LANE, running southwards across what was the Northmoor village common ('Airs Green'), was recorded from the 17th century. The riverside hamlet of Moreton (i.e. 'settlement in swampy ground') was mentioned from the early 13th century, and in the 1700s comprised a line of farmsteads straggling along the southern edge of the large central common and up towards Noah's Ark, some of which, such as Seldom Seen and Ramsey Farm, were described in the first chapter.

A few yards in from the northern end of Moreton Lane a public footpath leads down to the Northmoor Jubilee Wood. Commenced in 2012, the project formed a major feature of the village's celebrations commemorating the sixtieth anniversary of the coronation of Queen Elizabeth II. The village was selected by the Woodland Trust to receive 800 saplings – sufficient to create a spinney large enough to provide a wildlife refuge amidst the open fields towards the river. Over two autumns, sturdy volunteers including a pleasing number of children donned their wellies to plant a mixture of blackthorn, hawthorn, hazel, silver birch, rowan and common oak on a plot of land kindly provided by Graham Shelton (below right) and his wife Julia. Bribery in the form of hot drinks and homemade cakes ensured a gratifying turn-out on both occasions, and two sparkling autumn days only augmented the collective sense of smugness.

Flood is an ever-present threat in the Moreton area, but hopefully a good number of the brave little saplings will make it through to be appreciated by future generations in the same way that, today, we cherish the majestic trees planted in Northmoor by our forebears.

Graham Shelton

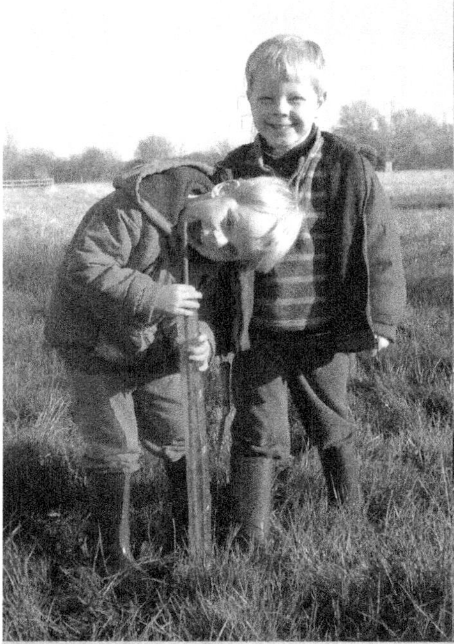

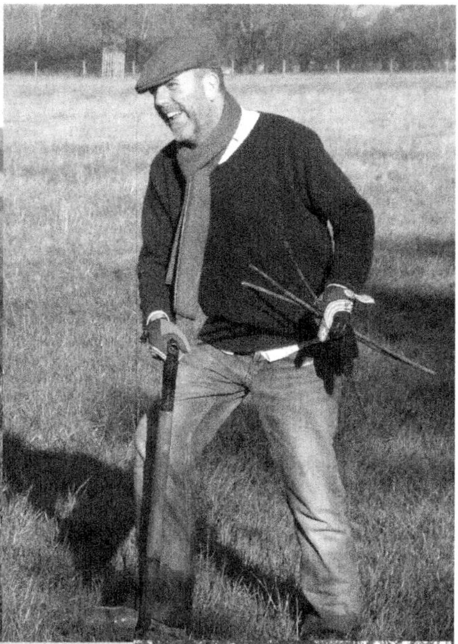

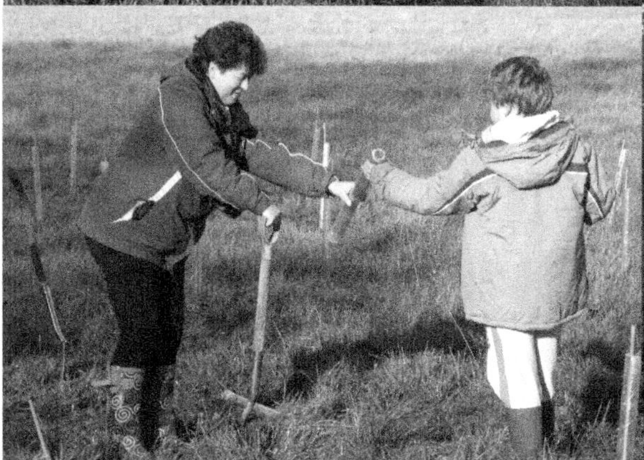

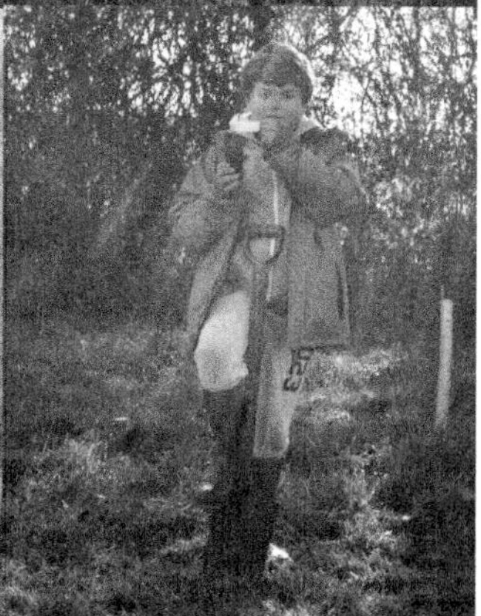

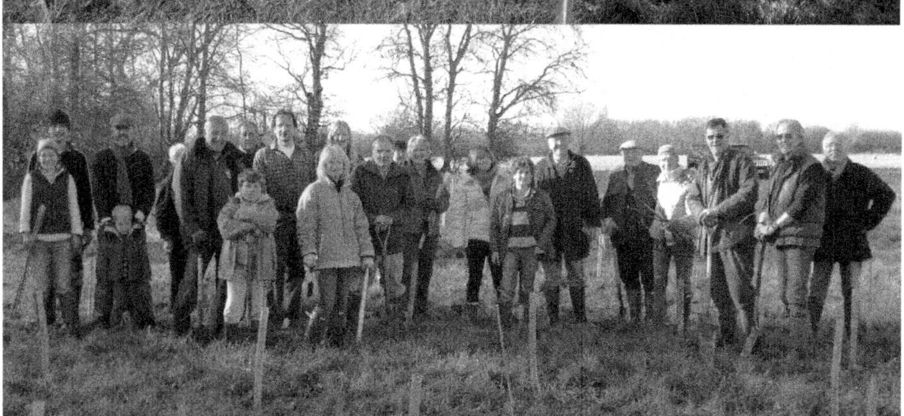

Magdalen College acquired Stonehenge Farm in the 1740s, selling it off in 1920. The Boston family farmed at Moreton during the 1960s, with the talented Graham Wren, who took many of the evocative images in this chapter, as their cowman. In 2010 residents fought by means of a public inquiry to oppose gravel extraction adjacent to the farm. They were ultimately unsuccessful, and it remains to be seen what impact the decision will have on this quiet corner of the parish.

Stonehenge Farm in the summer of 1965

Above: A member of the Boston family enquires how long dinner will be at Stonehenge Farm in the summer of 1965

Left: Walter Trafford, the roadman from Sutton, photographed in Moreton Lane in the summer of 1966

Spring 1964: David, Belinda, Nicola and Jonathan Boston

There may formerly have been a small green at the southern end of Moreton Lane with houses on its west and south sides, though by 1721 the site seems to have been divided into closes held with adjoining tenements. The hamlet's size altered little between the late 18th century and the late 19th, when there were around 16 dwellings, some dilapidated, and most occupied by labourers. Seventy-four of the parish's 375 residents lived in the busy hamlet of Moreton in 1851.

Moreton Farm at the hamlet's eastern end (below) included only farm buildings in the 1920s, and by the later 20th century the only houses were Stonehenge Farm and a few nearby cottages, some of them modern. Other farm buildings have now been converted for domestic use.

Charlie Williams, cowman for Tom Florey, chopping logs at his cottage in Moreton Lane in the winter of 1966

1960s

1970s

1990s

2013

Originally Moreton Lane ran down only to the river and along to Bablockhythe, but in the mid 19th century the track just south of Stonehenge Farm was replaced by a new 30-foot road running westwards to New Bridge. Charlie Williams, cowman for the Florey family, lived in a humble brick cottage built in the local style on the lane in the 1960s (opposite, below). The little cottage was modernised in the following decade, transformed into a Spanish-style hacienda during the 90s, and has now become the grandly-named 'Moreton House'. One wonders what Mr Williams would have thought of it all.

The Rose Revived inn at Newbridge was an alehouse by the later 17th century. Variously known over the years as the Chequers, the Barge, the Rose, the Rose and Crown and now the Rose Revived, it was leased in 1704 to one Augustin Rudge for 11 years, including three and a half acres of land adjacent to Newbridge. By 1753 the lease was in the hands of Augustin's son Joseph. And by 1771 the pub had been taken over by William Hutchins, assisted by his wife Zipporah.

Below: the Rose Revived in the 1890s

2011

In the 1970s lucky Raymond Blanc was given his first job in England as a waiter at the Rose Revived

New Bridge was probably built in about 1250 under the auspices of the monks of Deerhurst Priory, to whom the manor of More belonged. At the beginning of the 12th century, the Cotswolds wool trade was burgeoning and the revenues it raised were increasingly important to the royal finances. Communications

> **Short Notice of Sale on Wednesday Next.**
> MORETON, NORTHMOOR, NEAR WITNEY.
> 12 Acres of GROWING CROPS of Wheat, Barley, and Beans (all to go off), on lands late in the occupation of Mr. R. Florey, deceased,
>
> TO BE SOLD BY AUCTION, By Mess JONAS PAXTON & G. CASTLE, At Mrs. Wright's, the Rose and Crown, Newbridge, on Wednesday, Aug. 18, at Three o'clock in the afternoon. The Crops may be inspected at any time previous to the auction, and the customary credit will be allowed thereon. Catalogues can be obtained at the place of sale; inns in the locality; or of the auctioneers, Bicester.

1890s

2011

1791

1895

Today

89

between London and the wool towns were poor, and it became an economic necessity to build roads and bridges to speed the wool to the south. Building in stone had largely fallen out of fashion after the Romans left Britain, and only monasteries would have had access to the necessary expertise, which may explain the cathedral-like pointed arches which are a feature of this and nearby Radcot bridge.

The 'New' in New Bridge may be in relation to Radcot bridge, the original of which was built about 50 years earlier. Longer than Radcot, and built of superior stone from Taynton near Burford, New Bridge presently has six arches over the river and six in the causeway to the south. It seems to have once been much bigger. According to John Leland, writing in the 1540s:

'I rode then 2 myles and half through fayre champayne ground, fruitfull of corn to New Bridge on Isis. The ground there all about lyeth in low meadow, often overflown by rage of rayne. There is a long causeye of stone at each end of the bridge. The bridge itself has 6 grate arches of stone.'

More details were given in an account of 1692:

'New Bridge on Bark Shire side has 17 arches to ye main bridge. The bridge itself has six arches, and is about 53 paces or yards. Over on Oxford Shire side beyond ye main bridge are 28 arches, the causeway on Oxford Shire side is about 300 yards, and ye causeway on ye Bark Shire side 373 yards. And in all over causeways and bridge about 726 yards over 51 arches, to vent water in great flood.'

Writing in March 1659, local antiquarian Anthony Wood relates that when the bridge had fallen into disrepair in 1462:

'Several complaints were put up by the men of Kingston-Bagpuze and Stanlake for to have [New Bridge] repaired. Whereupon one Thomas Briggs, that lived in a hermitage at that end of the bridge next to Stanlake, obtained license to require the goodwill and favour of passengers that way and of the neighbouring villages: so that money being then collected, the bridge was repaired in good sort. This hermitage was a little old stone building, but beyond the memory of man it hath been an ale house, or pettie inn for travellers, called The Chequer. It belongs to Lyncolne College and Dod the tenant pays 3 shillings and 4 pence per annum for it by the name of The Hermitage alias The Chequer Inn in the parish of Stanlake.'

During the Civil War New Bridge was strategically important because King Charles I had set up his court in Oxford. On 27th May 1644 the Parliamentarians, commanded by Roundhead general William Waller (opposite), attempted to cross the bridge in order to surround Oxford and capture the king. Although they failed in this, it is said that Parliamentary troops did break down a section of the bridge in order to prevent the Royalists from escaping from Oxford.

According to Victorian photographer Henry Taunt, Waller then retired to Abingdon where he vented his frustration by destroying the beautiful market cross. Not a good loser, then. Eventually, however, the Parliamentarians prevailed in the bitter struggle and fortunately Northmoor's man of substance, Sir Edmund Warcupp, had chosen to fight on the winning side. Just as wisely, Warcupp then swapped sides to support the restoration of Charles II, and was duly rewarded with royal favour thereafter. Two annual fairs at New Bridge were granted to Warcupp in 1675.

From the later 18th century tolls were collected apparently by the lord's bailiff, but profits fell from around £13 in 1780 to 9 shillings in 1798. In 1806 the privilege of collecting tolls was let for 30 shillings to the tenant of the Rose and Crown, but though the fair house was mentioned in 1816 the fair itself had lapsed by the later 1840s.

By 1871 the coal trade through the wharf at the Rose Revived was thought to have declined since the opening in 1861 of the Witney railway, and the wharf finally closed in the early 20th century.

Roundhead general William Waller

Looking across to the Maybush at sunset

People *and events*

Seb Boston milking Jersey cow Naomi V at Stonehenge Farm in the 1960s

Frederick W Moss (1863–1951), shoe maker, at West End

Harry Calcutt and his son William Thomas

Above: Hannah Maria Hazzard Trinder (1846–1913). Above right: Hannah's husband James Trinder (1829–1901), a labourer. Below: Hannah and James's daughters Ethel (1886–1966) and Bertha (born 1884). Both girls went into service, Ethel in Woodstock and Bertha in St Clement's, Oxford

> Wm. Trinder, a native of Northmoor, was charged with being a deserter from the 1st Battalion of 20th Infantry, in which he was Corporal. The prisoner enlisted in 1868, and decamped from Exeter on the 1st inst. with 22*l*. belonging to the Government; remanded to await an escort.

Top left: William Trinder, his wife Elizabeth Walker, and their first child John. A corporal in the 1st Battalion, 20th Infantry, William was charged on 4th December 1869 with desertion (above). Could his departure from camp in Exeter on 1st December be connected to the arrival of his elder son, John (top right)? Four-week-old John William Trinder had been baptised in Northmoor on 21st November

Left: William Percival Trinder (1881–1957), younger son of William and Elizabeth Trinder. The long gap between the births of the boys suggests that William senior's case went badly, and by 1881 the former soldier is described simply as a 'labourer'

95

Above left: Nellie Henrietta Walker (born 1906) and Rose Lousia Walker (born 1907), daughters of George and Mary Louisa Walker. The Walker clan was large and complicated, with members in Standlake too. Above right: Little Rose Louisa grew up to marry William Talbot in 1935. Below: Thomas William Walker (1878-1953), son of George and Sarah Walker

1800

Water Supply and Fire Protection for Mansions, &c.
Merryweather & Sons.
63 Long Acre, London

1899

NORTHMOOR.

On Sunday afternoon a fire occurred on the farm occupied by Mr. Clifton at Northmoor, near Bablockhythe, by which a great deal of damage was done. It is supposed that the conflagration was caused by a spark from the chimney of one of two cottages near the farm buildings, and on account of the highly inflammable state of the thatched roofs, after the late hot weather, and the want of means to cope with the fire, the flames spread very rapidly, and involved the utter destruction of two ricks, barns, cart sheds, two hens with broods of chickens, &c., a cart and a trap being the only articles saved from the farm buildings. The cottages, also, were destroyed, but the occupants were fortunately able to save their furniture, which sustained slight damage by hasty removal. Mr. Clifton, who resides at Bablockhythe, is insured, but the landlord, Mr. Aubrey Harcourt, Nuneham Park, is uninsured. The Eynsham Fire Brigade arrived on the spot a considerable time after the outbreak, but were powerless to render much assistance.

1863

FIRE AT NORTHMOOR.—Shortly after midnight on Saturday, a straw rick on the premises of Mr. Packer, at Northmoor, was discovered to be on fire. A messenger was despatched to Oxford, and Mr. Goundrey without delay sent an engine with a pair of horses, but before it arrived the flames, by the exertions of the neighbours, aided by a plentiful supply of water, were extinguished. Several other ricks and buildings were in close proximity, but the fire was happily prevented from catching them. An incendiary is believed to have committed the act.

1899

NORTHMOOR.

George Walker and his wife, who suffered from the fire at Ferry Farm, Northmoor, on Sunday, the 4th of June last, desire to thank, through the medium of the public papers, all those who have so kindly subscribed to the fund raised for their benefit, also those who worked so hard.

George Walker 1868–1958

Harriet Walker 1875–1938

Jack Lay holds on to baby Fred while his other son John walks alongside. Mr Lay worked for Kyffin Florey at Manor Farm

Returning from Appleton woods during the Good Friday walk in 1951

Joan Ireland (right) and friends play in the churchyard in 1932

Elijah Ireland and his son Basil at Watkins Farm in the 1930s

Above and below: the once-traditional carnival parade

Right: Joyce Lay, later Douglas, wins the Ladies' Race

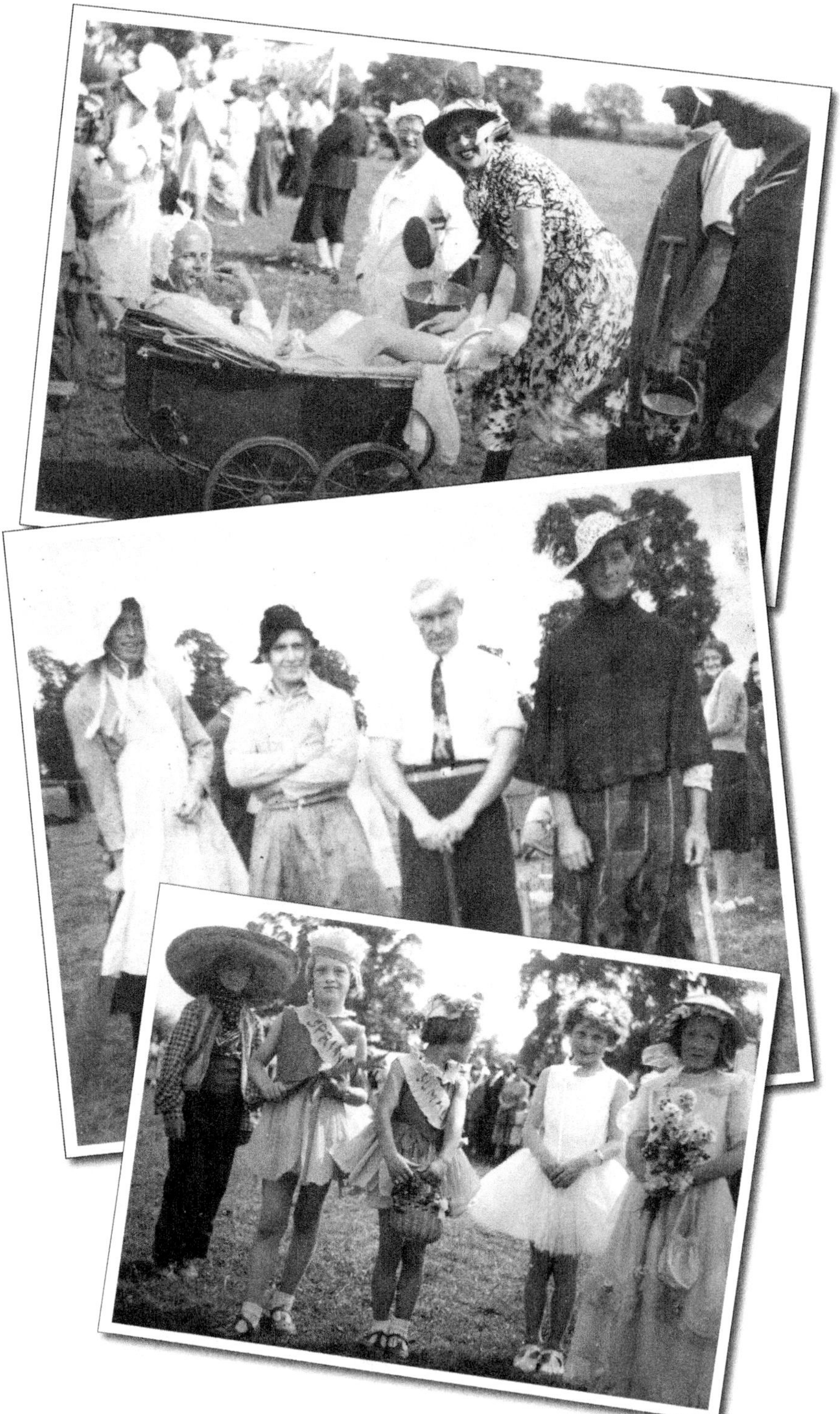

Opposite, top: 'Mum' Bernard Clack with 'Baby' Jim Hardiman in the 1952 pram race

Opposite, centre: Eric Sparrowhawk, Roy Douglas, Roy Wheeler and Stan Pullen dazzle in the Fancy Dress Cricket in 1950

Opposite, below: Children's Fancy Dress

Right: 1952 Carnival Queen Roseanne Palmer and her attendants Judy Webb, Val Bint, Bill Bint and Grenville Reeves

Above: Carnival Queen Margaret Pimm is attended by (left to right) Grenville Reeves, Judy Webb, Mick Lay and Yvonne Bint

Right: John Bruce invites champion boxer Randy Turpin to open the Carnival

101

Mavis Brooker (right) leads the maypole dancing in the school playground in 1958. To Mavis's right are Barry Sparrowhawk and Catherine Lay, and in the centre are Rosamund King and the Bint twins

Northmoor Sunday School, 1961

Apple Fair, 1974

The choir, Christmas 1997

2012 Jubilee Tea Party: Lisa Ellett (centre) and Mary Anne Florey serve Julie Thorne from the village's 40-cup Jubilee Teapot

2014 Superfast broadband switch-on: Graham Shelton introduces an excited PM, David Cameron

September 2015: Just when Cathy Price thought her national pub-crawl ordeal around 656 Red Lion Inns was over, she met Grenville Reeves

NORTHMOOR VILLAGE FETE & FLOWER SHOW
SUNDAY 24 AUGUST 2014
VILLAGE HALL • 2pm ONWARDS
Stalls • Games • BBQ • Bar • Teas

2015 NORTHMOOR
Village Fête
& Flower Show
Sunday 30th August
From 1pm:
Flower Show in the Hall
Fête at the Red Lion
Stalls • Games • Teas • Bar
BBQ • Live music

THE NORTHMOOR AND STANTON HARCOURT DRAINAGE BOARD.

Among the important advances that have of late been made in Oxfordshire in the improvement of land, there has probably been none so enterprising in its features and successful in its results as the embankment of lands against the floods of the Thames and Windrush which has been carried out at Northmoor and Stanton Harcourt.

The time was when Northmoor was so perennially wet and liable to flood that there was a sort of jocose idea that its inhabitants were born web-footed. This must now soon become a tradition of the fathers.

Mr. Harcourt, who has taken a very lively interest in the district where he is the chief proprietor, acting on a suggestion of some of his principal tenants, turned his attention to the possibility of keeping off the flood waters which had been every year the cause of such discomfort, inconvenience, and loss to the whole district. Mr. E. W. Harcourt entered most warmly into the proposal, and owing to these efforts a scheme was brought before the rest of the proprietors in the district, including St. John's College, the University of Oxford, Christ Church, and Magdalen College, and ultimately a Drainage Board was formed under the Land Drainage Act, 1861. Mr. Ripley, of Bracknell, was employed as the engineer of the works, and on the 25th of August, 1866, the first meeting of the Board was held, and the work was fairly begun. The embankment extends from Cut Mill farm on the Windrush, in the parish of Standlake, to half a mile north of Pinkle Weir, in the parish of Ensham, and is of a length of over six miles. It protects from the floods 2185 acres.

Several members of the Board, including Dr. Adams, Mr. Francis Field, Messrs. J. and S. Druce, Mr. Lord, of Stanton Harcourt, Mr. George Castle, Mr. Blake, and Mr. Geo. Watkins, and some other of the tenants and owners of land within the district, with Mr. Ripley, the Engineer, and Mr. Robert Hawkins, the Clerk to the Board, visited the bank on Wednesday last, for the purpose of making a final survey prior to the work being pronounced perfect and complete.

The view certainly impressed all with a most satisfactory confidence in the value of the work. The bank was in excellent condition, and had effectually resisted all the floods of the winter, notwithstanding the strong south-west winds which drove the floods in waves against it; while outside the bank the herbage was course, and made up chiefly of meadow sweet, reed grass, and marsh marigold, all grey with the mud of the floods of the last week. The grass within the bank, only separated from the other by the width of the bank and ditch, and exactly on the same level, has in the last two years become fine in quality, and presented the fresh rich green of upland meadows. Some of the grass fields within the bank were pared and broken up last year, and some are being pared and broken up this year, and in fact land that two years ago was and could only be poor grass land, liable to flood and damage at all seasons, is now made secure, and of certain and high value to owner and occupier, and capable of growing every kind of crop.

The day was bright and pleasant, and after the inspection was over all adjourned to the new buildings added by Mr. E. W. Harcourt to what was once the old Vicarage of Stanton Harcourt, and which is almost a part of the fine old buildings of the Manor House and Pope's Tower. Here a handsome dinner was provided by the chief landowner in the district, and the table was most tastefully set out with flowers, &c. Two noble salmon were placed on each of the tables, and were ready to be attacked as the guests were ushered in. Of the wines we need only say that they came out of the cellars of St. John's College, under the protection of Dr. Adams, who has been and is a most active member of the Board. Mr. E. W. Harcourt, the Chairman of the Board, presided at the dinner, and, after the usual loyal toasts, proposed "Success to the Northmoor and Stanton Harcourt Drainage Board," which was enthusiastically received. Mr. Grantham, the great authority on land drainage, was present, and expressed his high approval of the result of the work.

The Stanton Harcourt Church bells were rung out in full peal, and the party broke up about seven o'clock, delighted with the day's proceedings.

Above: 1869 – hurrah! No more floods! Below: 2014 (etc) – oops. More floods

© Billy McNeil

Prime minister David Cameron turns up to sort it all out

August 2013

January 2014

Same dog, different weather

Moreton Lane 2014

© Paul Fowler

No go: Church Road blocked at Watkins Farm

Ghost town: Thameside residents were evacuated

But mostly the river stays where it should be, like this…

… and this…

© Veronica Roth

... and this...

... and this.

*For further copies of this book,
please visit Amazon*

By the same author

THE WATER GYPSY: HOW A THAMES FISHERGIRL BECAME A VISCOUNTESS

AT DUSK on a snowy evening in 1766 a tired young couple made out the welcoming lights burning in the windows of the creaky old Berkshire manor house that was to be their home. He was Viscount Ashbrook, she was Betty Ridge, daughter of a humble Thames fisherman. Earlier that day they had been married in a little village church in Oxfordshire, and now Betty was embarking on a new life in the alien world of the aristocracy. But her beloved husband died young, and Betty was alone. Based on the author's original research, *The Water Gypsy* traces the previously untold story of Betty's struggle to protect her children's interests in the hostile climate of 18th-century Ireland. It was a project which culminated in the most glittering marriage in the entire history of the Ashbrook family when Betty's granddaughter became Duchess of Marlborough and chatelaine of Blenheim Palace.

ISBN 978-1784075545, price £10.99.
Available through bookshops, FeedARead.com, and Amazon.
Also available on Kindle.

www.julieanngodson.com

Also from Alley Cat Books

MEMORIES OF THE VALE
by Reverend Lewin G. Maine
Edited by Julie Ann Godson

FIRST PUBLISHED in 1866 as "A Berkshire Village: its history and antiquities", this little collection of memories and true tales from the Vale of the White Horse has charmed generations of readers. At a time of rapid change in the English countryside the author, Standord-in-the-Vale curate Reverend Lewin G. Maine, sought to record for posterity local people's recollections of a lost way of life. Now, exactly 150 years later, Reverend Maine's work has been given an extra lease of life in this new edition edited by local historian Julie Ann Godson.

    With more than 20 delightful period illustrations, the book takes the reader from the most obscure period of British history through to the final days of a truly rural existence before the Great Western Railway thundered into this quiet corner of England.

ISBN 978-1523690862, price £10.99.
Available on Amazon.
Also available on Kindle.

Printed in Great Britain
by Amazon